# YES YOU CAN!
## EVERYONE CAN SERVE THE LORD

### KEITH GILES

AMBASSADOR INTERNATIONAL
Greenville, South Carolina • Belfast, Northern Ireland

*Yes You Can!*
© Copyright 2004 Keith Giles

ISBN 1 84030 161 9

*Ambassador Publications*
a division of
Ambassador Productions Ltd.
Providence House
Ardenlee Street,
Belfast,
BT6 8QJ
Northern Ireland
www.ambassador-productions.com

Emerald House
427 Wade Hampton Blvd.
Greenville
SC 29609, USA
www.emeraldhouse.com

# CONTENTS

Introduction 7

## Part 1: Brief Encounters

1.  The Reluctant Servants *13*
2.  On the Road…*16*
3.  From Despair to Hope *19*
4.  From Co. Antrim to Ukraine to? *25*

## Part 2: Strengthening Supports

5.  Maintaining God's Kingdom *29*
6.  From Sickness to Service *33*
7.  Four into One does Go *35*
8.  A New Primary Project *37*
9.  Making a Difference *39*

## Part 3: On The Front Line

10.  Heartbreak and Hope *45*
11.  Putting Themselves in Danger *52*
12.  Never Say Never *55*
13.  Retire? No Way! *63*
14.  Caring Hearts *68*

15.    Spiritual Sight *75*

16.    Not Yet Finished *78*

17.    The Dunkirk Spirit *83*

18.    Not Florence Nightingale *87*

19.    Explore, Dream, Discover *91*

20.    Once Not Twice *95*

Conclusion *101*

Appendix *103*

*This book is dedicated to*

*My late father, without whose wise counsel I would not be the person I am.*

*My very living mother, who put up with so much during those teenage struggles – and we both survived.*

*My wife, Anne and children Rachel, Jonathan and Emma. You are all a great source of blessing from God to me.*

## Introduction

## YES YOU CAN!
### Everyone can serve the Lord

The Bible is full of accounts of God using ordinary people for His extraordinary purposes. Who would have thought that Gideon would become the leader and saviour of Israel? Remember John Mark in the New Testament; he deserted Paul and Barnabas on a mission trip but later became one of Paul's greatest supports.

God's 'selection process' is just so different to ours - Moses, Abraham, David and so on (see Hebrews 11 for the list of faith) - but it is Gideon who really intrigues me. Take another look in the book of Judges, chapters 6-8. There is nothing in Gideon that anyone in their right minds would consider to be noteworthy. He tells all to the angel in chapter 6 verse 15; he was from the least family in the weakest clan from the smallest tribe. It is how the angel of the LORD first addresses Gideon that gives a clue as to how God thinks of him – "The LORD is with you, mighty warrior." (Judges 6:12.[1])

God does not just look at us now, but what we can be if He is with us. As the LORD said to Joshua at the beginning of his leadership of the children of Israel, "As I was with Moses, so I will be with you; I will never leave you nor forsake you." (Joshua 1:5) This is one of the most precious promises given to the believer and it is

---

[1] All Scripture quotations from NIV unless stated.

repeated in the New Testament in Hebrews 13:5, with the added emphasis of "God has said"![2]

David made a statute in Israel that everyone, whatever their actual role, should share in the blessing, because first and foremost the blessing comes from the Lord (see 1 Samuel 30). When Paul speaks of the body of Christ in 1 Corinthians 12, not only does he explain, "God has arranged the parts in the body, **every one of them**, just as he wanted them to be." (1 Corinthians 12:18, my emphasis), he goes on in verse 22 to write "those parts of the body that seem to be weaker are indispensable".

Some of us still feel that that there is nothing we can do in the church or across the world to serve the Lord, and so the purpose of this book is to encourage everyone to re-evaluate their service and get involved where they can and where God has called them to be. The important factor is that God is with us, He sees what we can become with Him, not what we are now.

I remember when a friend approached the leaders of his church with a view to going to a Bible College, in order to get training to help to determine his call from the Lord. One of the leaders, rather smugly and very dismissively, said to him "We have all felt the call when we were young!" Implying that with time my friend would 'get over it'. It may be that you have felt the call of God at sometime in your life and feel that because you did not respond then, there is nothing that you can do now. That is not true – all of your experiences can be used in the service of the Lord.

Sometimes we forget that He is the same yesterday and today and forever and that the Lord still delights in taking ordinary people and using them for His extraordinary purposes. This book has been put together to encourage and motivate; many of the people you may never have heard of but God has used all of them because they were available and they obeyed.

I have tried to get a balance of ages, experiences, church backgrounds, mission organisations and countries of service. From

---

[2] I remember hearing a message from R.C. Sproul where he mentioned seeing bumper stickers with, 'God has said it, I believe it, that settles it!' on them. He comments that the middle clause is completely unnecessary - if God has said it - that settles it, whether we believe it or not!

time to time, it has not been possible to mention the exact country where someone is serving the Lord, due to the sensitivity of where they are and potential harm to their and others safety. That does not mean that they are under constant threat, but rather that there are still a number of countries where open displays of evangelism and conversion to Christianity are banned. Some of the chapters are quite short, because some of those I talked to did not feel that they had all that much to share – they too felt very ordinary – but that is the exact purpose of the book; God using the very ordinary.

At this point let me sincerely thank all of the people who took the time to speak to me – not all of them were very willing at first! I have tried to faithfully outline the information they gave me and so any errors are mine. Thanks are due to Sam Lowry and the team at Ambassador, who have been very kind and supportive. To Tom and Sylvia, thank you for your friendship over the years and Romania will never be the same again because of you both. Finally to Anne, thank you for your love, patience and support throughout the years and we pray together that our lovely children Rachel, Jonathan and Emma will grow up to serve the Lord.

You can be used by God for extraordinary acts no matter how ordinary you feel. With the greatest respect, I suggest that you read prayerfully and with an open and prayerful heart, because maybe you too are a Mighty Warrior, with the Lord!

# Part One

## Brief Encounters

You will receive power when the Holy Spirit comes on you; and you will be my witnesses in Jerusalem, and in all Judea and Samaria, and to the ends of the earth.

Acts 1:8

## THE RELUCTANT SERVANTS
David and Beth Cooper

Beth and David Cooper could well be considered a 'typical' Christian couple in Northern Ireland. Both brought up in Christian homes, David has been a member of the same church all of his life, Hill St. Presbyterian, and had been an Elder there too. Beth had been involved in the background helping and serving as the need arose. Their main emphasis had been bringing up their children. They were faithful and committed, vital in any church. They had supported the Presbyterian Church of Ireland (PCI) missionaries through the church, but had never ever thought of getting involved in missions themselves.

Even after they became friends with Tommy and LaVern Anderson, the local representatives of World Gospel Mission (WGM), there was no immediate desire to travel to other parts of the world, but it did deepen their interest in missions. They started to attend the monthly WGM prayer meetings and they watched the videos of Tommy's visits to various parts of the world. By this time their children had grown up, so it was easier to spare a few weeks and so as they got more involved, David suggested going on one of the work teams. Still there were doubts: "Would I be of any use?" was the first thought of Beth; she added: "I didn't want to be a burden."

Beth was not going to go at first to Honduras as she did not think that she could ever be of any use, but over time and after persuasion she did accompany David and a group of others to Honduras for two weeks in early 1999. One of the convincing factors came after they had met a missionary on furlough, Grace Appleby, who told them: "Please come – we love to see people!"

WGM teams are usually of a practical nature, supporting the on-going work of WGM missionaries in the area. In Honduras missionaries are running a school, whose buildings needed updated and painted. There was a language barrier, the local language being Spanish and so David and Beth mainly communicated with the missionaries; nevertheless the impact of the trip was immense: "You've heard about poor conditions, but when you've seen it for yourself…….." The sentence did not need to be finished. "It is an experience that you have yourself and you cannot bring it home to someone else."

There are some people that somehow you always know will get involved in Christian work or indeed, for example, were always going to be a teacher and so on. I do not think that anyone imagined David and Beth getting involved in missions, so I asked them how people had reacted after their first trip, whether people were interested to find out more. Their reply was fascinating: "People ask you, but do they really want to know?"

David feels that sometimes the missionaries and their organisations are partly to blame for a lack of interest back at home: "The information about what a missionary really does is not coming through. It appears that missionaries are just there to evangelise. All the information is needed." Now that is a challenge to the mission agencies! In the ever more competitive market for resources and personnel, the temptation is to make all the information glossy and exciting, when perhaps a healthy dose of reality is needed.

In 2000 the Coopers travelled to Momoniat, a village in Kenya where they helped to build a roof for the church. In a number of ways this was a far more rewarding experience as they were able to communicate with the locals who worked alongside the team, as many could speak English. David and Beth said that there was warmth and genuineness about the people in the villages as they fully appreciated the help that the team brought. As they were able to speak with the local Christians and other villagers, so the team were more able to understand their real needs and cares.

They returned to Kenya in 2003 to another area to again help to build and roof a church. They were able to revisit to Momoniat to renew fellowship and to see how the church was developing. Inevitably there were a number of events, place and people that remain in their memory after their two visits and you can tell that the people of Kenya now hold a special place in their hearts. One of the more poignant examples of the life in the village is that during the church services, when an offering is taken, it is not just money that is given, but also sugar cane, tea, rice etc., because some do not have any actual money but what they do have they give.

On trips like this it is customary for those going to pay their own way and the question is raised could the money spent on flights and so on not be better used directly by the locals? Are these trips just a waste of money? David answers emphatically: "No – for a number of reasons!" These trips benefit those who go on them; they are life changing – you are not the same as when you went, you get a different perspective on life at home and abroad. They are a benefit to those you visit practically in the case of WGM trips and also spiritually encourage the missionaries and local Christians, who can see the sacrifice that you are making giving up time, holiday and money to help them.

David and Beth Cooper are a living testimony to the change that going on a short term mission trip can make to themselves and to others. But we are still left with the nagging question that they asked: "Does the church (that is Christians) want to get involved?"

## ON THE ROAD TO THE MISSION FIELD
Jenny Mercer

Jenny is not a missionary yet....but I suspect that she will be. She has already visited Romania four times all for different reasons but each building up her determination to continue to seek the Lord's direction for her life.

Jenny was brought up in a Christian home and attended the local Church of Ireland, where she first cut her teeth in children's work. She has been exposed to stories about missionaries from her childhood and as she was growing up, thinking about what she wanted to do, she never imagined herself as being 'settled' in one job at home, but as yet there is no clear direction as to what the future holds.

She has just finished her Nursing Studies degree at Edinburgh University and has just returned there for a job after a few months in Romania. Whilst in Edinburgh she has attended Carrubbers Christian Centre and has been involved in running Christianity Explored courses and street evangelism. For Jenny her nursing studies have proved useful but more importantly her time in Edinburgh has strengthened her faith and she has learnt more about evangelism and obedience.

Jenny's first visit to Romania came in 1998, when she went on a cross-community school trip to orphanages in and around

Brasov. They all raised money and took out aid for the children. She enjoyed the times with the children in the orphanages, but overall was left with a sense that nothing lasting had really been achieved; that the physical aid was only a partial answer to the needs of the children.

The second trip came the following year, when Jenny went on a Gospel Literature Outreach (GLO) team to Talmaciu near Sibiu. She spent two weeks helping to run children's outreach clubs. GLO have missionaries based there who run a kindergarten and printing press. Interestingly, Carrubbers Christian Centre also has links with this town. Separately from the GLO work there is a Bible School, where members visit to teach and teams from the church go out to help to run summer Bible camps.

For her nursing elective as part of her course, Jenny returned to Brasov and worked for six weeks in a hospice. Romania was not her first choice, but every other opportunity that she looked at just did not work out. Often there would be no reply or she would get turned down. The hospice in Brasov is one of the better hospitals in Romania and, whilst is not exclusively Christian is definitely run with a Christian ethos.

Most recently, Jenny has just returned from three months based in Ghimbav close to Brasov, working alongside the local Baptist pastor and his wife. She is the sister of a Romanian that Jenny met in Edinburgh (who has since moved to Australia). Jenny worked in the kindergarten that is associated with the church and also got to know more about the work of Operation Mobilisation (OM) in Romania as their headquarters is in Ghimbav as well.

The three months gave Jenny more time to consider what the future might hold and she considered the place or area with the greatest need. In Romania often those with the greatest need are the gypsy communities; many of them are unreached with the gospel, rejected by the locals and lacking in basic education. Jenny also considered the need in health care and health education, particularly with her own training. Jenny is aware of the need for cultural sensitivity and recognises that within Romania there are many thriving and growing churches and that probably the most effective work that a 'foreign' missionary can do is to support the work already going on and encourage the Christians to grow and witness to all.

Jenny is thinking about what the future holds. There is a possibility that she will do some further evangelism training in London in the future, in the meantime she will gain experience in nursing and continue to serve the Lord in Edinburgh. At the moment she has no definite 'call' as such, but she can see the need and is available to follow the Lord's prompting as and when that should come.

# FROM DESPAIR TO HOPE
Paula Johnston

With everything that is happening across the world today, how could God call anyone to serve in Afghanistan? But that is where Paula Johnston spent six weeks during the summer of 2003. She was not blazing the trail of overt evangelism, there were no open air meetings, this was not a teaching and preaching tour but rather what is called 'tent making'. In many Muslim countries it is illegal to preach the gospel openly and so a number of Christian organisations use other methods to get the gospel into these countries; these include aid, teaching at schools and universities, teaching computer skills and as many other openings as they are able to use. Christians are there first and foremost to do their particular job of work but through friendship and the quiet witness, opportunities become available to speak for Christ.

Paula does not come from a Christian home, although her grandparents were 'good living' and this had an influence on her mum, who prayed with the children at bedtime and sent Paula and her brother to Sunday school. After a move to Glengormley, when Paula was about 10 years old, she befriended a girl called Julie at school, who invited her along to the Christian Endeavour Bible class her church. It was through this that Paula and her brother both became Christians, and although they did not fully understand what it all meant they knew it was the right thing to do.

Paula's teenage years were a struggle as she did not come from the 'perfect' family, who were not always supportive. Like many of a similar age, Paula also struggled with herself. She did not excel at anything academically or in sport; she was o.k. at most things and would have a go, but constantly felt that she was very ordinary. When she was seventeen she started worshipping at Glengormley Methodist Church and got involved in the Youth Choir as well as in youth club, but after she left school her circumstances changed and first she started work and then went to college.

She began a NNEB Diploma in order to become a Classroom Assistant, but when she went on a placement, she was soon disappointed that the job did not live up to her expectations. This only added to her sense of inadequacy and she left after a year. During this time she also started drinking, which was to cause some physical difficulties, but did nothing to take away her feelings.

In 1993 she joined the Civil Service as a temp and by this time her church attendance was minimal and her faith was a shambles. Alcohol caused a trapped nerve in her neck and so she faced a choice, stop drinking or lose the use of her left arm and so for around one and a half years she did stop drinking.

From then until the year 2000, Paula's life just gets worse and worse. Without going into graphic detail, she did attempt suicide and although Paula spent time with a Christian counsellor she did not feel that she got anywhere. She felt that she had no friends, no backing from her family and no God. By this time she had put all of her 'Christian' things in a bin liner – Bible, cross and so on. She doubted God's goodness; He was not a God of love, grace and forgiveness. "The sky was black" is how Paula describes those times.

Towards the end of 2000, Paula was beginning to suspect that the man she was involved with was married (he turned out to not only have children from his current marriage, but also from a previous marriage – and did not think it important enough to tell Paula), so she went for a walk to try and clear her head. As she was walking, advice came into her head as to how she should deal with the difficulties she was facing. She does not know how, but she knows it was God. She did not go looking for God, He came to her. She could see that God knew and understood all that she had gone through and was going through. It was not that all of her anger and despair did not matter to God, but that He stretched past it to reach Paula.

Paula describes the experience graphically. "It was like being a child again; when you've been separated from your parents in the supermarket and when they find you, they give you that great big hug." She wept as she stood in the middle of the street. The same God that she had embraced as a 12 year old was now embracing her again. As she looks back now, she can see how God had been with her all through those darkest days and she is amazed that she was still alive – but that was all down to God.

Paula admits that it was a few months before she went back to a church as she did feel let down by other Christians, but in February 2001 she started to go along to Glengormley Free Methodist Church. In May she was asked to help out with the youth club and soon afterwards Gordon McCormick from the Lisburn Free Methodist Church spoke about his involvement in Tanzania and Paula was challenged to go to the farm there. They were in fact looking for mechanics, but she went along in July and spent the time looking after Gordon's children, cooking, cleaning and sorting out all of the gifts of food that had been sent out.

On her return her Pastor suggested that she would benefit from going to Thailand in December that year to a missionary conference, in which the first week was a conference and training on mission and evangelism in Asia and the second week was spent in field exposure in a local hospital.

Meanwhile an interest in Afghanistan that had first kindled in 1991 returned. She knew that because of the situation any work there would be 'tent-making', still with no real training she felt that she could do that. As she thought about this, she wondered whether it was from God or just her own idea. She prayed about the whole situation and knew that God was leading her. She also knew that aid workers had been arrested there and tried to find out all about the organisations involved; she often met with a stone wall, but eventually discovered that it was 'Shelter Now' and 'People International'.

It was on September 11th 2001, a date which has been etched in all of our memories, that she first met with Simon Carter the local representative of People International. He told her of a scheduled sponsored bike ride across Asia, the following year, which would give her much needed exposure to the Muslim world.

She then went off to Thailand and it was there that she was first challenged to go to Bible College, at first she laughed the idea off, thinking that "it would be like being at church every day". The verses from Ephesians 3:20,21 were particularly significant to her at that time:

> Now to him who is able to do immeasurably more than all we ask or imagine, according to his power that is at work within us, to him be glory in the church and in Christ Jesus throughout all generations, for ever and ever! Amen.

As 2002 started, it seemed that everything was happening too quickly. She had only just returned to following the Lord and every step that she was taking was getting bigger and bigger and the cost of all of her activities was rising. It would cost £3000 for the bike ride and £3000 for Bible College. She had never been the most confident of people and wondered how others in the church would view things – as she appeared to be a relative newcomer looking for support and help for these ventures. A friend from India that she had met at the Thailand conference sent her an e-mail and shared with her verses from the Bible – which included Ephesians 3:20. She continued to seek the Lord for confirmation that what she was doing was what He wanted.

It is always difficult to describe how different people sense the leading of the Lord in their lives – a number of factors come into play; scripture, prayer, wise counsel of leaders and friends – and with all of this comes the testimony of the Holy Spirit. Romans chapter 8 gives a beautiful picture of the Spirit at work in us, encouraging us to set our minds on the Holy Spirit's desire, that is God's desire, (verse 5), the Spirit's testimony (verse 16) and the

Spirit's help in our weakness (verse 26). As we aim to keep in step with the Spirit (Galatians 5:25), so He will lead and guide us.

Paula was accepted on the two year diploma in Church Mission and Biblical Studies at Belfast Bible College, and they agreed to excuse her from the first three weeks so that she could go on the bike ride, by which time had been moved to Turkey for safety reasons. She had taken a career break from the Civil Service so that she could start the studies and so she was not able to take on any other employment to help to pay for the fees.

During the first year there are two placements, one in the UK and one overseas, both of six weeks duration. For the overseas placement there was an opportunity for another bike ride this time for Missionary Aviation Fellowship, but felt that she should at least look at the possibility of going to Afghanistan. After all it was her interest in Afghanistan that had caused her to go on the bike ride and to go to Bible College.

There was a lot of logistical difficulties in making the arrangements, organising the secondment to Shelter Now, the travel plans – even when she travelled there was problems as one leg of the journey had not been properly booked – and so on. But in June 2003 she finally arrived at Faisabad in northern Afghanistan, where she would spend the next few weeks. Faisabad is a remote area where even the Taliban had failed to conquer.

Her main task was to help tutor at the computer school that is there, mainly for local women who worked for non-governmental organisations (NGOs), so there was a good level of English spoken. They were fairly capable therefore it was not so much teaching as tutorial work and helping when they had problems and questions. It is not that the people there want to take on western values, but they realise the benefits of education and computers can bring.

Before Paula left for Afghanistan, she was warned not to speak openly of her faith or to engage in evangelism as this could easily be reported and ruin many years hard work by the charity and put some of the locals in danger. What Paula found was that the local people were more than happy to talk about western culture and compare it to their own, to ask about the U.K., to compare standards. They talked about faith and the Koran, they talked about Christ. This came up in ordinary conversation because for the Afghan people their faith and their lives are intertwined and not separated. Paula did not have to 'force' or twist the conversation around to matters of faith, they would come naturally.

Paula's pre-conceived ideas were changed too; after a few days there she became sick and it was the local men who would care for her, bring her food and ask after her health. There was an appreciation of the sacrifice that she had made, that she had left behind her comfort and friends, that she had given up her summer holidays to travel all the way over to Afghanistan to help them to learn more in computing skills.

Paula's future is less uncertain; she has resigned from the Civil Service knowing that she would never return there (sometimes it is easier to know what it is you will not do as opposed to what you will do), she is currently supporting herself through the second year of college by working with Age Concern, surprising even herself in her enjoyment of supporting older people. Paula has a tendency for impatience, wanting to know now what is going to happen. Through all of her experiences God has been teaching her patience, she is learning to trust God as she has been stretched by Him. She has also appreciated the support of her church both in small ways and in larger ways as the need has arisen.

I am sure that there are many who feel that they are inadequate and unskilled and could never serve God; that they do not have the gifts of evangelism. Perhaps you feel that God could never use you because of the depths you have been to, because of what you have done as a Christian, how far you have slipped away. Paula's testimony is that God gives gifts and opportunities to even those who fall and to those who feel inadequate; He can bring them back and through all of their experiences lead them to a place where He can use them. You may not have to travel to Afghanistan, but pray that God will direct you to where He wants you to be.

# FROM COUNTY ANTRIM TO UKRAINE TO ?
Stacy Todd

A nurse – now that's a 'typical' missionary vocation. Throughout the history of missionary work God has called nurses; mainly, although not exclusively, female, to serve across the seas. So be careful, if you are a nurse then watch out!

Stacy Todd is a nurse and she was the first from Northern Ireland to work with World Gospel Mission (WGM) in the Ukraine. (Tommy Anderson, the local Director and Jim Clarke, who is on the WGM council, had visited to see what was going on previously). For two weeks, Stacy worked alongside the WGM workers helping out at a local church with the youth work, based in the southern coastal city of Berdansk. For a number of years a couple from the USA have been establishing a work in that area. They have helped found three local churches, with one local pastor and are engaged in a number of other support activities including the youth work, general outreach and clothes distribution. They have purchased a derelict building, which was the local drug haunt, and are in the process of getting refurbished in preparation of the opening of a local Christian centre in order to help the work progress.

Their next venture is to develop a Mobile Medical Unit. There is little effective health care across the country. In the capital, Kiev, there is widespread tuberculosis and various other bronchial conditions, as well as many problems with alcoholism. The unit would have a doctor and nurse, an x-ray machine and aim to train in health management and dentistry. The plan is to buy and adapt an articulated lorry and take the unit around the villages, using it as a base for reaching out into the communities. Inevitably with Stacy's qualifications and experience, the local workers hope that she will return to get involved.

Stacy is unsure of her future. She hopes to get married soon, but she does believe that she and her fiancé will end up on the mission field, but she does not know where. Stacy was not brought up in a Christian family; in fact her mother is from a Catholic background and her father a Protestant, which adds to its own difficulties. She went along to a local CEF Good News Club, when she was very young and she was saved when she was just six years old. Due to her background, there was little encouragement and so she did not go along to church.

Incredibly, her mother got saved as a result of door-to-door outreach from the local Baptist church and so they both started to attend that church. It was there that she really started to learn about the Bible and what the Christian life was all about. A friend took her along to Abbott's Cross Congregational church and she began to get involved and grow effectively as a Christian. Over the next four or five years she helped out in summer outreaches, Good News Clubs and 5 day holiday clubs; for Stacy she was learning to reach out in her own neighbourhood.

She has been thinking about missions for a long time. As she said, "Where would the desire come from, without God's call?" After a youth fellowship initiative on missions, she contacted WGM through the internet, hoping to go to Central America; but this outreach was only for Americans – so they put her in touch with Tommy Anderson, the local Director and Stacy ended up going to the Ukraine. As mentioned previously, whilst Stacy thoroughly enjoyed her time in the Ukraine and valued the experience and exposure to mission that it gave her, she is not sure of her next step. But she is open to the leading of the Lord and has a desire to serve the Lord, wherever He calls.

# Part Two

## Strengthening Supports

God has arranged the parts in the body, every one of them, just as he wanted them to be.

1 Corinthians 12:18

## MAINTAINING GOD'S KINGDOM
John and Jennifer Young

What is it about nurses that God uses? Is it that because by nature and profession they are involved in caring for people that they see the needs of the world for effective Christian care and the gospel? Jennifer Young is another person involved in mission that trained as a nurse. She had a 'normal' Christian upbringing in Co. Down, getting converted as a child and growing in her faith as she grew up. She got involved in the youth fellowship at church and also helped out on a Gospel Literature Outreach team in Northern Ireland. It was whilst she was at Nursing College that her life changed completely. She went on holiday to America and there met John Young, a farmer, from Illinois.

John was also from a Christian home and although became a Christian at a young age, it was not until his early twenties that it became real. He had also helped out on a mission team (in Mexico) and had been a leader at summer youth camps for a number of years. A couple of years after they first met, John came to Northern Ireland to seek out relatives who had emigrated from Co. Down in 1924. It transpired that John's relatives knew Jennifer's parents and John stayed at Jennifer's house during his stay.

Love blossomed and after a three year courtship they got married in 1992 and went to live in the United States. Their first child, Fiona, was born in 1996 and Nygell was born in 1998. John continued his work in farming and Jennifer began working with a Rescue Unit in Illinois. They attended John's home church which is best described as a conservative Baptist Church.

After their previous experience both John and Jennifer had the desire to help out in short-term missions. In 1995, their church was organising a trip to Haiti for a ten-day trip to assist missionaries already serving there. At that time there was unrest in Haiti and so the numbers reduced down to three; John, Jennifer and Mark, a church friend. As there were only a few in the team no major project could be undertaken so John and Mark did maintenance jobs around the missionary compound; what they discovered is that often mission stations have plenty of offers to help with a building project but there is no-one able to maintain the finished work. For example, taps were broken in the kitchen which meant carrying water in from outside; John and Mark were able to fix those so that time and energy could be saved and running water again was available. Jennifer helped out with the day to day living such as going to the market and providing hospitality. By the end of the trip, both John and Jennifer realised just how much practical skills are needed in missions and that back-up personnel provide a vital role in support-ing the 'front-line' missionaries.

Some time later, in 1998, a couple from Wycliffe Bible Translators came home on furlough and as they belonged to the same church as John and Jennifer, a friendship developed as John and Jennifer explored possibilities of missionary service. The couple suggested being involved in the support side of Wycliffe called Jungle and Aviation Radio Service (JAARS). This service provides the back up to the translators so that they can get on with their main task of translating the Bible. Wycliffe was the first mission agency that John and Jennifer came across that had a full-time dedicated back-up team. All the others that they had looked at, a mission worker would have to be a speaker first and maintenance came second; but John realised that his skills lay in maintenance and not in public speaking.

John and Jennifer continued to pray and went along to the local Wycliffe office in Chicago for an interview, which resulted in a year-long application process. This included a week of technical evaluation in North Carolina to determine where John's skills lay. It became clear that John was best suited to the Construction and Maintenance department (CAM). Towards the end of the application John, Jennifer, Fiona and Nygell went along to the mountains outside Los Angeles for a further opportunity to discover more of the work of Wycliffe and the processes involved in the translating of the Bible into various languages and dialects. They also learnt about the changes that missionary life would bring to the family. After further interviews John and Jennifer were accepted into the Wycliffe family in March 2000.

On their return to Illinois, they undertook a variety of Bible correspondence courses through Moody Bible College, whilst John worked to raise support so that they could begin their training in North Carolina. In January 2001 the family set off for the JAARS centre for an intensive five month programme before entering the mission field. As they came towards the end of their training, a decision as to where their first assignment was going to be had to be made. During their time there they had been preparing for the Philippines, but the Lord led them to England to work at the Wycliffe Centre in High Wycombe, Buckinghamshire for a period of four years.

The centre was initially purchased in 1972 as a summer school of Linguistics and at the time it was just used during the summer months. In recent years training has become more geared individually to the missionaries own needs and so there is now training all the year around, and people come to stay from between 3 weeks to three and a half months. Extra space at the centre is used for conferences and the like.

Wycliffe is a completely faith-based mission organisation; none of the missionaries receive a salary; once they had sold their home and raised their support they moved to England in November 2001. Initially, John was the Building Maintenance Supervisor, which progressed to manager and now he is the Estates Services Manager. He oversees all of the construction and maintenance teams as well as all of the grounds and gardening teams. Jennifer works on a part-time basis in the residential services department which entails helping with the flats in the centre, working on the internal mailing system – receiving and distributing mail to all Wycliffe workers and maintaining a database – and working in the boutique, which has second-hand clothes donated for missionaries. Fiona is now seven and Nygell is five and have both settled into a local school and the family live in the centre as John's duties include weekend work.

They have now reached the halfway stage of their service in England and thoughts are already starting to move towards where the Lord would have them serve next. At the moment their intention is to return to the JAARS centre in the U.S. and see where there is greatest need at the time when they complete their service in England.

Is there an easy answer for knowing if there is a right time to go into missionary service? John and Jennifer believe that the Lord will reveal that to your heart and he will prepare you for what He has called you to do. They also believe that there is not a skill or job that people do that God cannot use in missionary service. And so that means no-one is excluded. If you hear God's voice – do not harden your heart!

# FROM SICKNESS TO SERVICE
Alan Kennedy

"If you had seen Alan a year ago, you would be very surprised to see him here now" is how I was introduced to Alan Kennedy who is acting as a part-time administrator for Project Evangelism. For around five years Alan suffered with ME and was forced to leave university where he was studying Radiography. Alan had become a Christian around the age of 11 and attends Dundrum Methodist church. His mother is a Christian but his father is not. His life is fairly unremarkable, although he did feel as he was growing up through his teenage years that he should be living 'better' than he was.

His illness caused him to rethink his faith. He prayed for healing, but it did not come. He began to doubt that God even existed. He searched the internet and had every question that he could think of answered and again became convinced that Jesus Christ is real. He did not receive any healing but now as far as Alan was concerned his faith and Christian walk was based on fact and not feelings.

In May 2001 Alan began playing the guitar at praise and worship services to at least get himself out of the house and through the encouragement of Mark Wallace, who was at that time over from the USA working with Project Evangelism, started to help more and more at Murlough House. As part of his recovery process, he is permitted to work a number of hours as therapeutic experience and continue to receive Income Support.

Alan still hopes to return to complete his radiography course, but he realises that no plans of his are set in stone but trusts the Lord to continue his recovery process and to lead him where He wants. In the hands of the Lord, even a serious illness cannot stop people from serving Him.

## FOUR INTO ONE DOES GO
Sally Patty

Every Christian organisation needs 'back office' staff, helping in all of the administrative needs. This is one area that is often forgotten about. An administrator in a Christian organisation regularly works 'solo' without the support of others in the administrative team, as perhaps you would find in similar sized secular organisations.

Sally Patty has worked for the International Federation of Evangelical Students (IFES) for a number of years and 'does the work of four people', but the rewards are that 'no two days are the same'. There is the mundane work of accounts, filing and taking minutes and Sally admits that there are times when you feel isolated, the only interaction with other people seeming to be on the telephone, but at other times – in the run up to conferences and newsletter deadlines and so on – it can be manic.

In IFES, there is a weekly team meeting, so Sally is able to develop real relationships with the other field workers. She also leads a summer team to Moldova, goes along to conferences and is the minute secretary to the Student Council, so there are opportunities for her to get hands on experience of the work that IFES is involved in.

Sally was brought up in a Christian home and became a Christian at a young age. When she went to Jordanstown, she got involved in the Christian Union and was a small group leader, a committee member and was the Irish Representative on the Student Council; so she was familiar with IFES and its work. After leaving college she worked for seven years as an Academic Researcher, before being asked to work with IFES. Sally, like many administrators in similar positions, does get paid a salary, but this would not be the level that she could expect to earn in the 'outside world' and so she, and her husband, (she only got married recently) are making sacrifices for her to be able to fulfil the administrative role for IFES.

Administrators, like Sally, are often prized possessions in mission agencies, as the pay could be zero or little, and the public profile even less, which makes support raising very difficult. But they perform such a vital part of the work, often co-ordinating all of the publicity as well as other important tasks. Like most administrators, they are often under-valued until they are not there!

We usually think of a call to mission being all about the direct evangelism, the church planting and the like, but it is essential that God calls administrators and similar to His work. Pray that the Lord of the Harvest will send workers – in all areas of service.

## A NEW PRIMARY PROJECT
Irene Maguire

"We could not achieve what we do without a reliable secretary" so said John Moxen, the director of Project Evangelism concerning Irene Maguire, who at the time was very reluctant to talk to me. Irene felt that she was 'too ordinary' to be included. I told her that she was exactly the type of person I wanted to talk to.

Irene has been a churchgoer all of her life. She was a member of the local Church of Ireland in Dundrum and although she read the Bible, she felt that she was good enough to get into heaven. Then Rev. Sam Brennan was speaking at the church when Irene was about 30 years of age on Revelation 3:20; that Jesus was knocking on the door. It was then she realised that she was not good enough and she asked Jesus to come into her life.

During the early nineties Project Evangelism moved down from Portrush to Murlough House in Dundrum and started to build up relationships with the Christians in the village. Brian Russell was the minister of Dundrum Church of Ireland, with his wife Esther at the time and they were very supportive of the work in the early days. Irene too, would help with suppers and the developing women's ministry at Murlough House.

Irene continued to work as secretary in the local primary school as she had done for many years, with never a thought of being involved more fully at Murlough House. She worked with the women's fellowship at the church and was an active member of a prayer group. After many years at the school she was finding the ever rising demands tougher and tougher to bear and eventually handed in her resignation due to stress. After about four months, she met Jo Moxen, John's wife, and offered to help out if needed, without realising what the consequences would be.

One day some time later, Irene was in Newcastle to go to the job centre to apply for a classroom assistant job, when she met John and Jo. "I could do with a secretary" said John and so Irene went along for an interview and agreed to work for a three months trial, four mornings a week, four hours a day. At the end of the three months, John pleaded "Please don't leave me!"

Irene does not feel much like a missionary, but the work that she does is vital in ensuring that evangelism is done in the towns and villages in South Down and other parts. For Irene it was all about the Lord's timing and He is faithful to supply all the necessary details. She does receive a small salary but again not commensurate with all the work she does!

Continue to pray for Irene and those like her, who quietly and efficiently co-ordinate the administrative and secretarial work of mission agencies. They are basically irreplaceable!

## MAKING A DIFFERENCE
Jim and Elva McBratney

In Acts 13, the Holy Spirit sets apart Paul and Barnabas for mission-ary work; significantly they were part of the group of leaders and teachers in the church at Antioch. Today, we tend to think that it is only young people who would be called to go to the mission field, wherever that may be, rather than those who are holding or who have held leadership positions. On reflection, those with experience of church leadership, running Christian organisations or similar would be ideally placed to help and train others who are just starting out.

After 20 years in the pastorate, in 1987, Jim and Elva left their relatively comfortable surroundings to work alongside New Tribes Mission (NTM) across the world. For ten years they travelled to America, Australia and England training, teaching and helping to prepare workers for the field. From its inception NTM has been a pioneering missionary organisation, aiming specifically to take the gospel into unreached areas and tribes.

Their interest was kindled during the time that their daughter, Heather, and her husband were missionaries with NTM in Senegal. After they had visited them in their location and saw the work and the impact that they were having in the villages, they felt the call to serve with NTM themselves, using their skills to prepare others for the work, at the various NTM training centres. It was not that their congregations were unresponsive, but they wanted to have a direct impact on the spreading of the gospel.

NTM have over 3000 missionaries, involved in all aspects of the work. Consider this example; when Heather and her husband were in Senegal, because of the remoteness of their location EVERYTHING that they needed had to be flown in. That entailed a buyer to buy and pack all the provisions, a pilot to fly the plane to the various locations, an engineer to ensure that the plane was airworthy and so on and so on. In order to keep two missionaries in the field there is a whole backup team with a variety of skills working often unseen by the churches. Without this support team, the missionaries would have to journey a long way to get their own provisions and this would necessitate a two week absence from the tribe on a very regular basis.

No-one who serves with NTM receives a salary – all live by faith and all are considered missionaries, whatever their actual duties as all are part of the team and network that is taking the gospel into those unreached area. Jim's role was largely defined – teaching in the Bible schools. Elva's role was far more varied – acting as secretary to Jim, helping to prepare the NTM magazine, receiving and selecting articles from all NTM missionaries of their work, looking after those who came to stay at the centres and so on. During their ten years with NTM, they also visited Papua New Guinea and helped out on the Interface programme, a three month intensive training course designed to give new workers direct experience in the field - as Jim and Elva told me: "Whatever you may feel – you can make a difference."

In 1996, they returned to Northern Ireland and took up the pastorate at Rosemary Park Baptist Church in Bangor, where they have served up until October 2003 at which time they retired. Is now the time for them to settle down and take a well earned break? By no means! They are now back in England based at the NTM centre in Lincoln, helping out wherever they can. Their presence there has enabled a younger man, a skilled linguist to be released to return to the field.

With so many people far more active in their retirement in these days – and with the variety of opportunities that there are to serve whatever the skill, more people could follow the McBratneys in using their retirement as an opportunity to draw on their skills and experience to serve the Lord, wherever He may call.

In times past we may have felt that mission was best done by 'the young'. However more and more mission agencies are using older, wiser and experienced Christians to spread the gospel across the world. There has always been a difficulty for missionaries with the education of their children, which has often meant that they have had to return from the field, sometimes never to return. Those, whose children are older and have left home, could use their skill and abilities to serve the Lord in a variety of ways both in the front line, as it were, and in support ministries at home or abroad.

# Part Three

## On The
## Front Line

Go into all the world and preach the good news
to all creation.

Mark 16:15

## HEARTBREAK AND HOPE
Wilson and Irene McMahon

After 15 years of service in the Philippines with Overseas Missionary Fellowship (OMF), Wilson and Irene McMahon with their family are on long-term furlough back in Northern Ireland. They are settling back into life with Wilson undertaking a course of study at Union Theological College and Owen (16), Anna-Claire (13) and Gavin (9) have all settled reasonably well into local schools. They served for the most part in 'unreached' areas and have seen the work there grow and develop.

Many of us would be happy with that succinct summary of the McMahon's experience. But it does no justice to what they really have been through. In the introduction I explained that this book is meant to be an encouragement but it cannot be sanitized from the reality of the hardships that sometimes go hand in hand with serving the Lord.

Irene comes from a Christian home and grew up in a Presbyterian church, where throughout her years was exposed to missionaries and mission work, through reading biographies and visits to the church and home. To her, the stories that she heard indicated the 'heroic' nature of missionaries but as she more fully learnt what missionaries were involved in, she began to realise that she wanted to be a missionary.

"Church was boring!" So said Wilson as he was growing up; coming from a non-Christian home and sent to church as a youngster he could not wait to get to the stage where he would not have to go there anymore. Something made a difference – it was a Bible Class teacher called William Rea, an older man, not in any way modern or up-to-date; but someone who was worthy of respect, who believed what he said and who showed genuine concern for the young lads under his care. It was a long process before Wilson became a Christian at the age of 18, but it was part of a tremendous work that God did in his family as other close relations became Christians both before and afterwards.

Irene was already a member of 1st Antrim Presbyterian Church, when Wilson joined. The minister there, John Dixon, was the chairman of the Irish Overseas Missionary Fellowship (OMF) council and so mission had a high profile within that church family. Wilson and Irene worked together in the youth club and have found it to have been good mission preparation, having to relate to all sorts of people from a variety of backgrounds. It is as they continued their work in the church and as they became more and more exposed to mission that Wilson asked himself the question, "Does God want me?"

Their church had a mission committee which helped them work through the process of their desire to serve the Lord. Wilson started at Belfast Bible College in the autumn of 1984 and Irene a year later. During the summer of 1985 they got married. They found the whole experience of Bible College useful in that they learnt principles that proved vital in their future service and they learnt to interact with Christians from different backgrounds. Further to this they experienced living by faith at home before they ever went abroad and saw how God provided for their needs during their time at college.

They had felt that God was leading them to work in a Muslim country and as part of the college year Wilson spent a couple of months in early 1986 working with a church in Bradford, England which is a city that has a large Asian population. Whilst appreciating the opportunity to learn it proved to be a frustrating experience as there was no opportunity for direct evangelism due to the approach of the church and its leaders. It became clearer that with many of the mission agencies that operated in the Muslim world, if, as Wilson felt, your gift was in preaching then there would be limited opportunities.

The following year both Wilson and Irene had to go on a field trip. Wilson this time went to the Philippines with OMF to a centre that operated as both an agricultural and Bible training centre. Irene, who was six months pregnant, spent those two months at the OMF headquarters in Sevenoaks, Kent. These months helped to confirm their call to work alongside OMF as Irene in particular benefited from seeing 'behind the scenes' and seeing first hand how OMF went about supporting missionaries, she saw the prayer and the passion and she saw how God provided for over 300 missionaries across the world, mostly not with large gifts but with small donations sent in from people across the land.

Owen was born in May 1987 and Wilson completed his studies just afterwards. He then spent a year working alongside the late Rev. Howard Lewis at Belvoir Presbyterian Church. As Irene collected her diploma in 1988 so they were accepted into OMF and moved across to the International Headquarters in Singapore in April 1989. Singapore is unique in its location as a bridge between east and west; a highly westernised city/state alongside traditional Chinese, Malay and Asian enclaves. For eight weeks Wilson, Irene and Owen learnt about OMF and the 'east'. Leaving home can prove to be a daunting step; leaving families and relations behind can be a tremendous wrench and the McMahons experienced much of the trauma of separation – in their own words they were 'grief-stricken'.

The McMahons then moved onto the Philippines to spend a couple of months learning the native language in Davao. OMF had been working with tribal groups for twenty or so years and had developed a significant ministry in the country. The following year in 1990 their second child, Anna-Claire was born in Davao. Towards the end of that year they moved with Owen and little Anna-Claire into the tribal area of Bukidon/Nasuli and began to learn the Manobo dialect. The move was not without its difficulties, for many months

Irene was almost constantly sick, not with particularly serious illnesses, but with a variety of ailments.

Working in 'unreached' areas brings with it its own difficulties. They are difficult to reach geographically, with little or no effective transport or roads; there is no electricity or running water; survival is based on what you can grow or carry. Unreached often means that the people have not been reached by government agencies – perhaps there is no effective rule of law, no schools, no post offices, no health clinics. To mission agencies, particularly OMF, unreached means fundamentally that the people have not yet heard about the good news of Jesus and that is why families like the McMahons suffer the lack of amenities that many of us have become so accustomed to, in order to bring the gospel to these areas.

For their first term in the Philippines the McMahons were working by themselves and the impact that they had was small. Then early in 1992 something happened that changed the way that the local people felt about them. Irene had become pregnant again during 1991 and it had been a difficult one. On January 15th 1992, Rebekah Joy was born in the Bethel Hospital. She died nine hours later and is buried in the grounds. This tragedy helped the villagers to relate more to the family as many of them had also lost children. In their minds nothing bad ever happened to the white people who used hospitals. Indeed after a period of recovery when Irene returned to the village there was an outbreak of pneumonia which resulted in the death of some of the children in the village.

The Bethel hospital is a hospital with a Christian ethos about 70km from the village that the McMahons lived. Its facilities were similar to those in our hospitals in the 1940s but its care was second to none. Often missionaries would go home, but the hospital was most appreciative that the McMahons trusted the doctors and nurses enough to have them care for Irene. This was further emphasised by the fact that when Irene became pregnant again in late 1995, again there were difficulties but Gavin was born in March 1996 at Bethel Hospital.

During the pregnancy in 1991, Wilson had become ill with Dengui fever and needed a transfusion to aid recovery; with no-one in the village able to take him to the hospital, the McMahons prayed that someone would come to the village, but no-one came and so eventually Wilson had to take the motocross bike and travel the tricky journey to the hospital where he received the necessary treatment.

Despite all of these traumas and heartaches, Irene and Wilson did not become angry or embittered but continued to trust in the Lord and as they look back to those tragic days they see rather that it was a strategic turning point in their ministry in the Philippines. During the months following their return to the village they further developed the work in Kalagangan and Talupakan.

At the time OMF missionaries usually served four years in the field and then returned home for one year, engaging in deputation as well as recharging the batteries as it were before returning to the field. For Irene and Wilson their planned return to Northern Ireland in 1993 was somewhat rushed as Irene's father was taken ill and was given only a very short time to live. They left in such a rush that did not have a chance to say goodbye either to those around their tribal home nor the lowland base. As it turned out Irene's father rallied and lived for a further year and at least Irene was able to spend those months with him.

The children settled well, Owen attended primary school and for Anna-Claire this was her first taste of Northern Ireland life. However the deputation meetings became increasingly difficult. The more that Irene and Wilson thought about this, the more they realised that everyone is faithfully praying for them but no-one is praying for the Manobo people. So over the year, 30-40 people committed themselves to pray for the Manobo tribe and for the work while Irene committed herself to writing regularly to their prayer partners with information and updates.

On their return to the tribal areas they managed to establish churches and a Bible School. The training centre functioned as a Bible teaching centre for the lay leaders of the local churches but also as a practical agricultural training centre. In the same year that Gavin was born an Australian couple, Mark and Susan Chapman, joined them in their work in the remote villages.

After their second home assignment, the team grew even more and over the last three years they have been joined by a couple and three single people from the Philippines and one girl from Malaysia as well as others previously to that. Wilson's main responsibility grew to be the team leader guiding and directing the newest members. In 2002 the McMahons had to move to Manila. The decision was a difficult one because the work was growing at a tremendous pace and it was heartbreaking to leave the newly formed team. Wilson continued to fly south to direct affairs and fulfil his obligations but the team was forced to develop quickly. It was a time when God was preparing this new multi-cultural team for when the McMahons would leave the country altogether and God has used the team in an amazing way. This was a particular blessing for Wilson and Irene who for so long had been by themselves and that sense of loneliness had been very wearying.

During 2003 the McMahon family returned to Northern Ireland for an indefinite period of time. The children have settled well back into local schools. Wilson is studying for a B.D. As they look back over their years in the Philippines they have found the whole experience of missionary service satisfying and enriching. Clearly they had a sense of adventure as they moved around in these remote villages and they have seen parts of the country that the tourist will never see. In order to be effective Wilson and Irene consider that it is important to take an interest in the country and culture as a whole and not just to be focused on the 'spiritual' work. Finally the McMahons recommend that you do not take yourself too seriously!

After 15 years of service the McMahons are looking for other challenges, almost certainly within the mission field. They have sacrificed much and gone through pain and heartache. They have been separated from 'civilisation' and other missionaries. But they have seen God richly bless their ministry and have seen the work in that part of the Philippines develop with a multi-cultural team now working in many areas of Mindanao. It is true that currently they miss the work and the focus of being involved directly in God's service overseas, but they are waiting for God's leading and direction for the next part of the adventure.

The life of missionaries is not always easy and sometimes they suffer pain and trauma as the McMahon family have done over the years, but we can be assured that whatever God calls us to do, He will give us the grace to be able to cope with all that life throws at us Don't let the fear of the unknown stop you from responding to God's call. The McMahons certainly do not claim to be super Christians, instead only those who have followed the leading of the Lord in their lives. You can too!

## PUTTING THEMSELVES IN DANGER
Mark and Louise Jones

We have all probably read or heard heroic stories of the adventures of missionaries in the nineteenth and early twentieth centuries; where the truth is that when they left these shores many never returned, giving their lives in the service of the Lord. We often do not like to consider the risks that many Christians still face today. Christians are persecuted throughout the world in greater numbers than at any time in history. Being a missionary can be a risky business, but if that is what God wants you to do, then it is a risk worth taking.

Mark and Louise Jones planned to leave Northern Ireland during the early part of 2004. Because of the nature of the work that they are going to be involved in and the location, it is prudent that those things are not mentioned. Why? As there are many dangers that Christian workers, foreign and nationals, face in certain parts of the world and in order not to compromise their safety, it is best not to mention everything to everyone.

But why would a recently married young couple be prepared to leave their families, their work and their home to live in a foreign land for an indefinite period, putting them in potential danger? Simply because they believe that their Lord has called them to and He has promised never to leave them.

Both Mark and Louise have Christian parents who have encouraged them to get involved in all kinds of Christian work. Louise became a Christian at four years of age and grew through attendance at Good News Clubs and Girls Brigade. Mark became a Christian at 13 at a school Scripture Union weekend. They also had the benefit of being under the ministry of Rev. Tom Shaw, who had worked for the Faith Mission before moving into the ministry. He encouraged people to experience missions and there were regular exposure to various mission agencies through the missionary weekends. Around a dozen or so families from the church were involved in missionary work and so missions were not something strange.

When Louise was just thirteen she went to Belarus on an aid trip with the Eschol Trust, which was an eye opening experience to the needs in another part of the world. She spent her summers throughout her older teenage years working with Good New Clubs, and spent much time working with CEF in 5 day clubs. Mark too trained with CEF in Co. Sligo and ran children's meetings. He visited Kenya on holiday to see his sister who was spending one year there with Africa Inland Mission. It was a challenging holiday, where he saw the needs of the people and also saw missionaries in their 'every day lives' – in his words "they were more normal than I thought!". He has also spent two weeks in Croatia on a practical mission trip.

Ever since Mark and Louise have been going out they have talked about being involved in mission work and in the year they got engaged, 2000, they went with SIM to India, in a sense to test the waters, as an opportunity to gain some cultural experience. They went in a support role, to meet missionaries and nationals and find out what was going on. On their return they continued to work in the church in Sunday school and youth fellowship.

As they continued to work with the youth fellowship they wanted the young people to find out more about missions and looked at various opportunities to share with the YF and as they did so their own burden increased. As they say, "We got itchy feet, itchy hearts and itchy minds." As they continued to pray about possibilities, they talked to their minister, listened to tapes and read the Bible and books. Through all of this, with the challenge of Scripture, they looked into how they could get involved.

They realised that the skills that they had acquired through work as well as all of their direct Christian experience are useful skills in today's world. As plans were made so they shared their vision with their parents and the church and along with them, their parents, their minister and the missionary committee all supported them in prayer. Inevitably there is some concern by their parents due to where they are going, but like Mark and Louise, they have faith in the Lord and are secure in the knowledge that this is the will of the Lord for them. For Mark and Louise it is this 'team' of prayer that gives them that added reassurance as to what the Lord wants for them. "Everybody is working together."

## NEVER SAY NEVER
Iain and Heather McKelvie


Iain and Heather have been married 10 years and have two children, Philip who is 7 and Debbie who is 3. After they got married, they settled down to some sort of 'normal' routine. Before Philip was born, Heather continued to work as a secretary. They worshipped at Bloomfield Baptist and got involved working in Sunday school and Campaigners. Heather's sister was a missionary with Operation Mobilisation and, at a missionary conference, Heather saw a vacancy for a secretary working with another missionary organisation and because that was her skill, she asked and was told that practical skills are needed on the mission field too – not just so-called spiritual vocations such as evangelism and preaching! She was challenged by God but did nothing about it and soon got back into the swing of day to day life. Meanwhile, as Iain continued to grow as a Christian he had put together a list of 'NEVERS' that he would never do: He would never go to Bible College, never go to Peru and never be a Pastor in Northern Ireland. With his background and skills, none of them were likely so he thought he was o.k.

Iain comes from a non-Christian background, but his is a story where with hindsight, it is clear that God has been guiding Iain to the place where he became a Christian. Iain was sent along to Sunday school until he was about 12, when at the first opportunity he left. However over the next year or so, his two best friends at school became Christians and were always talking to Iain about his need of salvation. Even after he left school and got a job, he discovered that one his work colleagues was a Christian and whose life, in Iain's words, 'just shone'. After that Iain met Heather at a Young Life meeting in Belfast and as a result of all of God's working in his life, he did become a Christian.

Heather, on the other hand, was brought up in a Christian family in Newcastle, Co. Down and became a Christian when she was 8 years old as a result of being witnessed to by a native from Zambia, who was in Northern Ireland for outreach work. As she grew up she became involved in the local Young Life group and as a result was trained and encouraged to get involved in witnessing and evangelism. After leaving school, Heather moved to Belfast and worked as a secretary.

After Philip was born, Heather gave up work and Iain continued to work at the Blind Centre. Iain had left school with no qualifications but they still had enough money coming in to survive without the two incomes. When Philip was about one and a half, Iain decided that he wanted to 'better himself' and get some qualifications, by leaving work and going to college. Heather admitted that she wept bitterly and at first was very reluctant to agree – she was worried about money, about Philip (who was going to look after him?), about returning to work. They prayed and asked God to confirm that what was being planned was in His will, they asked Him to provide a job for Heather. She was so surprised when, at the very first interview, she was offered the job that she turned it down!

Heather joined a temp agency and got work that way, Iain began an Access course at Castlereagh College, where there was a crèche for Philip. Iain planned at this time to apply for a Social Work course in the future, as he had worked with them during his time at the Blind Centre and so was aware of at least some of the requirements.  When the time came he was interviewed to go onto the Social Work degree course on one Monday. He felt that he had done well up until the last question, which was: "Have you ever been discriminated against and how did you cope?" Iain answered that he felt that he had and he just got on with it and did not let it get him down. When the result of the interview came through on the Friday, he was turned down. He was very angry and could not believe it. Maybe he would have been better to have answered that last question differently, such as, instead of accepting discrimination, he should have fought against it.

Maybe there was an ironic twist in all of that; if he was discriminated against, because he did not answer a question on discrimination to their liking, perhaps God was encouraging Iain to react as he said he did in the interview, by just getting on with life. In the end, that is what happened. Iain had been starting to think about going to Bible College, but had put it to the back of his mind as he was concentrating on going for the social work course. Now that door was closed firmly in his face, the Bible College option came back to his mind. (This was the first of the 'NEVERS' that God had overturned.)

Iain was accepted on to the two year course at Belfast Bible College, but when they were visiting the college, Heather was told that wives were expected to get involved in study as well. She was not expecting that - a full-time job, a toddler and to study one night a week and the extra commitment that that would entail. Providentially, there were a number of Christians working in the same place as Heather and they provided the encouragement that she needed. It was certainly difficult adjusting at first, but eventually she did settle down.

For Iain's first 'field' assignment, he had arranged to work alongside Dessie Creelman of the Northern Baptist Association in and around Northern Ireland with the book trailer, at churches, country fairs and so on. Around Christmas they had been given an anonymous gift of £500 and had agreed to put it to one side as they did not need it at that time. Dessie came to Iain before the start of the assignment and told him that there was a slight problem, he had been asked to go to Peru to speak at camps during the summer. (Dessie had previously been a Missionary in Peru with Baptist Missions). Iain did not think this was a problem as the assignment was over before the summer. However, as Dessie pointed out – the seasons are the other way around, its summer during our winter and he had taken the liberty to book two tickets, one for him, the other for Iain. The cost? £515. To Iain and Heather this was clearly God's provision – He had provided for all that they needed even before they knew they needed it! The parallel between that and God's provision of a Saviour long before any of us knew we needed Him is obvious.

So as part of the field term, Iain went to Peru for three weeks and spent the time with Dessie helping out in children's work and camps. (This was the second NEVER that God overturned.) Iain came back from that experience 'fired up' and enthusiastic for Peru, a feeling which Heather did not share. By this time Heather was self-employed and doing secretarial work for Stephen Wright at Young Life and when Debbie was born gave up the college studies.

Iain added a Spanish course during his second year and as part of his continued studies, another field trip was planned to travel with European Christian Mission to Spain. However three weeks before he was due to leave he fractured his ankle playing football, which meant that he was housebound and could not put any weight on his foot for seven weeks. Inevitably it proved to be a difficult summer adjusting to the circumstances, but for Iain it gave him an opportunity to read a wide variety of Christian books that he had never had the chance or inclination to do, including Church History by Eusebius!

After he recovered from his ankle, Iain was due to speak at a meeting but had to cancel because of a sore throat. It turned out to be quinsy and he was in hospital for four days. Usually the inflammation is lanced but Iain's was too close to his main vein and could only be sorted out through antibiotics. It has left Iain with a weakness in his throat, which will always be susceptible to further illness.

It was becoming clearer that God was leading them to be involved in mission, they had been praying more and more and God had been answering their prayers. Through the accident and illness it had meant that Iain had not had the opportunity to go to Spain and so Peru was the only country that Iain had been to. Baptist Missions served in Peru, but was mainly a church planting and Bible teaching ministry at the Seminary. Heather and Iain felt that the Lord had given them different skills. They renewed contact with Roy Gamble of Serving in Mission (SIM), whom they had met before. SIM have an international ministry which included Peru, where they worked with street children.

Iain and Heather had both worked previously with special needs children, had been involved in children's work at church and in their words 'had children in their hearts'. It was not that Iain and Heather had any particular 'special revelation', rather that over the years, through the ups and downs, through difficulties and easier times, God had been working in their lives 'directing their paths' (see Proverbs 3: 5,6).

It is usual for missionaries to go out for an initial period of two years with SIM; for Heather and Iain it was recommended that they went for two months after Iain graduated in order for them to experience the work as a family and to get better acquainted to what was going to be expected of them.

In all of the preparations and assessments that need to be taken, prior to any final decision, one is the effect on the immediate family and relations. Heather's father and stepmother (her mother had died when she was 5 years old), were now living in Wales and were supportive. Heather's father had often thought that he would become a missionary, but like King David's desire to build the temple, it was his offspring that was to accomplish that. Iain's parents are not Christians and after his initial trip to Peru, were not in favour of the idea of them 'taking away the grandchildren'. As time has passed and they have seen the type of work that they will be involved in, their reaction now is, "If that's what your God wants then so be it."

Iain and Heather have experienced the 'white knuckle ride' that often accompanies those who live by faith; that is that finances are often only available at the last moment, testing faith to the limit sometimes. Prior to their two month family trip to Peru, they prayed that God would provide the necessary finance well in advance. They had received enough by early May; Iain graduated at the end of the month and they left at the end of June.

The two month trip gave the McKelvies the opportunity to experience almost everything that life in Peru was like, such as power and water cuts and earthquakes. For Iain, it was very different to his previous trip because of the added family responsibilities. They travelled around various centres in Lima, Abancay and Arequipa, and it was in Arequipa where they felt the Lord say: "Welcome home!" They also visited with Baptist missionaries in Tacna, where they gained even more confirmation from the Lord that Arequipa was the place He had for them.

For Philip and Debbie it was something completely different, whilst Iain and Heather tried to stop them playing in the puddles, (there are no buildings that are public conveniences), the children thoroughly enjoyed themselves and stayed remarkably healthy. Philip is looking forward to going back in 2004 permanently.

On their return, everything has been set in motion for their return to Arequipa to help with the work there. In the meantime, Iain was asked to help out at Downpatrick Baptist Church. The Pastor was going to be away for a few months – so he handed the keys as it were over to Iain. (The third NEVER has now been overturned by God.) He found it a great learning experience working with a relatively small church and they valued their time there.

Peru is a country with around 26 million people and Lima the capital has around 10 million. According to the World Health Organisation 119 children die every day in Peru from malnutrition and other preventable diseases. 95% of children have primary education but this reduces to 40% who experience secondary education. The country is dominated by the Andes mountain range and experiences every possible climate within its borders. The south of the country is an earthquake zone and they had a major one in the summer 2002 and are expecting another one soon, to correct the fault in the earth that was created by the last earthquake.

Arequipa is a city with a population of about 1 million, with desert mountains on one side and volcano mountains on the other. A German family called the Reuters have been running the SIM children's ministry in Arequipa for 11 years. 26 churches are involved in the programme where 2000 children are fed before school 5 days a week; the breakfast consists of porridge, bread roll and milk. Many of the children keep the roll for their lunch. As part of the programme there is also a Bible class every day, where the children learn verses and are taught Bible truths.

Their parents are also included in that, in order for their children to be part of the programme they have to attend a monthly midweek service, where an informative lesson on healthcare or education is given and a summary of what the children have been learning, as well as the gospel being preached.

The Reuters are a nurse and mid-wife and so their main area of interest and care is in the health promotion side of the work. Because of the numbers involved they are unable to keep up with the entire medical programme. Heather will help relieve the burden of administration and Iain will help with visitation. Other areas of the work include Bible teaching and ministry training as up to 90% of local pastors do not have formal theological training, but are able to go to Chiguata Bible Institute for courses on a part-time basis.

There is also a camp site in the mountains, an 'oasis in the desert'; where up to 100 children can be housed at a time. It only costs 25p per day for each child, but most cannot afford it so as they come from farming backgrounds they 'pay' by bringing potatoes or lambs and so on. There is no running water – it is got from the well and neither is there electricity and it gets dark at 5pm so lanterns are lit until 8pm and then everyone goes to bed and get up the next morning at 5am.

The McKelvies are planning to travel to Peru in the early part of 2004 and are thoroughly looking forward to getting down to the work that is involved. A comment that Iain made is significant, because these are no 'confident in their own abilities' type of people, but rather those who are trusting the Lord and are seeking to follow what He wants for their lives. Iain said: "Sometimes I have to pinch myself, to think that God is actually using me!"

Considering the background of Iain and Heather, there is nothing particularly remarkable to make them stand out as outstanding missionary candidates against anybody else in the church. In many ways, with a young family, it would mitigate against going abroad. They have suffered their fair share of setbacks and difficulties. But they have been willing to follow where they have been led by the Lord, even if sometimes somewhat reluctantly. Now that they are about to embark on their journey to Peru, they pray that God will go before them and continue to guide and protect them and perhaps as a result of their witness someone else will follow the Lord's call to service, whether at home or abroad.

## RETIRE? NO WAY!
Mary Steele

"If I have one regret, it's that I did not get to Ghana earlier. I was already in my early thirties when I arrived." That is what Mary Steele says. Yet it was in 1962 that she went to Ghana and she had already been involved in Christian work for around 10 years! But such is her commitment and dedication to the work that she has been involved in since then, that she wishes she could have started before 1962.

Mary was brought up on a farm just outside Ballymena in a Christian family, with a long heritage of service in that there were at least two generations of Presbyterian Ministers. She became a Christian while she was at primary school around the age of nine and started to dream about becoming a missionary after reading about the exploits of Mary Slessor and David Livingstone. Visits by missionaries to her local church further strengthened her desire to serve on the mission field.

Around the age of 16 or 17, she decided for definite that she would train as a nurse in order to go to the mission field and at 18 moved to Belfast to train first in general nursing and then to specialise in midwifery. Following a period of time she went to Labrador with a mission called the Grenfell Mission and served as a missionary nurse for about three years.

She had long had the desire to serve in Africa and the chance came to go to South Africa to work in a Church of Scotland Mission Hospital, her particular skill in midwifery being very useful. However, as she helped all of the people she began to realise that all of the various ethnic groups had no Bible in their language. Mary wanted to do more to help them and so she left South Africa and returned to Glasgow to go to Bible School in order to get a better grounding in the Scriptures. Whilst she was there a Wycliffe Bible Translator came along to talk about the work – and in Mary's words – 'everything just clicked'. This is what she had been looking for. During the first summer vacation, she went on a linguistics course run by Wycliffe and she was accepted to join Wycliffe towards the end of 1959.

She returned to finish her studies at Glasgow and then went for three months on an orientation trip to Mexico, called 'Jungle Camp', where she was taught how to build a shelter in the jungle, how to make a bed from straw and how to make an oven from mud. Finally in November 1962, Mary arrived in Ghana.

She first went with a co-worker to North-Eastern Ghana to the Konkomba people; who had no written language. Together they began the task of living with the people, learning from the people and learning the language in order to form an alphabet. Mary's co-worker had to leave after one term because of ill-health and for a while there were a few temporary co-workers, but for the most part Mary has been by herself in Ghana working on producing a translation of the Bible into the Konkomba language.

When Mary first arrived there were six struggling churches that did not have much interest in getting the Bible translated – after all they had survived without one for years, but once the New Testament was completed in 1978, there was a lot more interest and a firmer foundation of faith.

As Mary looks back she praises God for the way that He has transformed the lives of the Konkomban people. There are now many more churches, many more Christians and no longer is there a fear of witchcraft. Their standard of living has improved, as their literacy rate has increased and they have learnt to use their money more wisely.

Mary continued working on the Old Testament and in 1998 the whole Bible was published and dedicated. The New Testament has been revised and now the people of Konkomba have the New Testament on tape and the Jesus film has been dubbed in to Konkomban.

After translating the first New Testament in 1978, Mary began working on the Bimoba language of a nearby people's group. The New Testament was ready in 1987 and in November 2004 the whole Bible will be published and dedicated.

Whilst Mary said that she has not faced much opposition throughout her time in Ghana, since the people in general are very friendly; she has felt the lack of fellowship over the years, although when she lived in the village the Chief was a Christian. In the earlier years communication with the 'outside world' was more difficult and so she was more isolated. Travel by road was difficult as over the initial period the road network deteriorated, but more recently has improved. At one stage she had no transport and waited by the edge of the road all day waiting for a passing vehicle. It was then time to get a small motorcycle to ease the burden.

In 1983, when Mary was back in Northern Ireland on furlough, there was a coup and the pastor ands his wife survived by eating roots and leaves in the bush for six months and once before Mary did have to be evacuated, but in general the political situation has been relatively stable.

Over the years Mary has had various bouts of sickness, but nothing so serious that she has had to consider leaving. She has suffered among other things from malaria, but she has always felt keenly the prayers of those back home, particularly from her home church, Killymurris Presbyterian.

Mary now works as a Translation Consultant, checking translations currently being undertaken and giving advice. She returns to Ghana each year and comes back to Northern Ireland only during the rainy season. She is now based in Tamalee and does have more contact with the other missionaries. Translation has moved on since Mary first began in the early sixties and often local people are trained to translate which speeds up the whole process.

When someone with Mary's long experience on the mission field, not just in Ghana, but also as a nurse in Labrador and South Africa, gives some advice, it pays to listen to it. Mary says: 'If God is calling you, then go ahead as He will provide the enabling and the training.' Mary recalls her own background, living and working on a farm and then, initially after leaving school, moving into secretarial work. After that she trained to be a nurse and set off for the mission field before the call to change direction came as she started her service with Wycliffe as a Bible Translator.

We do not always have the skills and abilities when we begin our journey of service, but as God's plans are revealed so we learn and progress. Mary was willing to serve and through her dedication and her heart to see others have the ability to read and study the Bible in their own language, God challenged her to change direction.

When Mary joined Wycliffe she expected it to be a lifetime commitment. Her first goal was to translate a New Testament into a local dialect, however long that took. After that to translate the whole Bible, then she moved onto the next language starting with the New Testament and finally the whole Bible. She continues to encourage and help others as more and more local dialects receive the Bible in their own language. Her view is simple, 'I have never had a call from the Lord to come home!' So she stays.

It does not take a professor of mathematics to work out that if Mary was in her thirties when she first reached Ghana in 1962 that now she is in her seventies. She still has a heart to reach out to the people of Ghana and so she will carry on. Her life has been totally dedicated to the Lord and she is an example to many. She is almost a legend (she would hate to think that) for having translated two complete Bibles and dedicated over fifty years of her life to mission and is highly respected and liked by the local people of Ghana as well as the wider missionary family (and not just those associated with Wycliffe).

Mary Steele is an example to us all, almost as it were, a throw back to the old time missionaries who left these shores never really expecting to return, but willing to give their lives in total service to the Lord whom they love. May Mary be an inspiration to us all. Remember she started out as a nurse and has become a renowned Bible translator. What can God do with and for you? Are you willing to take a step and find out?

## CARING HEARTS
Simon and Sharon Carter

"I only wanted to go kayaking and canoeing!" but Simon ended up hearing the gospel for the first time, when because a Christian camp offered those water sports, he went along. He had been brought up in a non-Christian home in Taunton, Somerset (having been born in Bournemouth), and as his mother was the school secretary, she opened all of the post and knowing of Simon's love of water sports let him know of the opportunity.

He was prepared to put up with the Christians so that he could experience the canoeing and kayaking. While he was there, he was 'persuaded' to become a Christian – at least to say the right words – by a well-meaning leader and so when he returned home, he tried to 'be' a Christian by doing all of the right things. He read his Bible, prayed (the prayers he learnt at school assemblies), but did not go to church as his previous experiences had been so boring – but there had been no change of heart and so as hard as he tried, it did not work. He could not keep it up.

Later on an English teacher invited a classmate of Simon's to a youth group at the local Anglican church and he took Simon along. The youth leader was very 'earthy', in that he did not always behave exactly as a Christian should, but nevertheless, preached and lived the gospel; he was extremely caring and accepting. For the first time, Simon understood the gospel message, responded and became a true follower of Jesus Christ.

He got involved with Don Double and the Good News Campaign and experienced a tremendous filling of the Holy Spirit and, whilst he recognises now that he was a 'pain in the neck' to his work colleagues (he was working in the local Council offices) due to his over-enthusiasm, it was a time of Simon being on-fire for the Lord, seeking to tell others about their need of a Saviour.

When he was 18, in 1982, he read an article in the Observer Magazine about starving children in Africa. He was deeply moved and complained, "It is not fair, Lord!" He got a reply that he was not expecting – "What are you going to do about it, Simon?" As a result he went to Kenya for one year with Africa Inland Mission (AIM) from 1983 – 1984.

His main responsibility was as a book-keeper at a hospital and he also ran Bible studies for the nurses. With another Christian he was also able to visit the patients in the hospital and spend time with them, praying with them as appropriate. It was not an easy time and Simon even had the heartbreak of having a young starving child die in his arms.

At that time Simon had no formal training, but was willing to go because he felt that the Lord wanted him to. It was a time where he felt that God had used him like never before. He really 'clicked' with the Kenyans and enjoyed the experience of working and living in a different culture.

On his return, he wanted to learn more. Not knowing which college to attend, the two names that kept cropping up were All Nations and Moorlands Bible College. He applied but was turned down – not enough qualifications for All Nations and, he later learnt, not the right attitude for Moorlands.

Sharon, on the other hand, was brought up in a devout Christian home and her parents were committed, active members of Armagh Gospel Hall. Sharon became a Christian at the age of 11 at a 'wee' mission held in the locality and continued to develop as a Christian.

When she was nearly 18, she went to the Ulster Hospital to train as a nurse and joined the nearby Brooklands Gospel Hall. There she got involved in leading the youth work and started to put together a programme for the youth to pray for the missionaries that were associated with the church. There were about five couples who were serving the Lord in various places and Sharon started to pray in particular for one couple, with whom she kept in regular contact and found out a lot more about their day-to-day routine. Through all of that the Lord began to speak to her of her need to get involved. As a single young woman, Sharon realised that there was nothing holding her back.

It was in 1985, after qualifying and working as a Staff Nurse that she went along to a prayer meeting and a man told of a need that missionaries working in Zaire had for a nurse. She took a leaflet about them and their work and began to pray. When she visited home in Armagh to tell her mother of what she was thinking about, her mother gave her the very same leaflet about the work in Zaire. For one year, Sharon worked in a very isolated area in Zaire, with only the two missionaries and the local people. It was hard but rewarding. In a veiled compliment the lady missionary told her, "You're a bit stupid, but have a lovely smile!" The (hidden) implication being that the African people loved Sharon.

That year confirmed to Sharon what she felt the Lord wanted her to do and on her return she took a midwifery course in order to be even more useful in mission hospitals, as many of the patients are there for pregnancy related issues. She then went to Moorlands Bible College.

Simon had not forgotten about his desire to serve the Lord and, after working in an estate agent's and also in a local village in Somerset where a group of Christians from his local church bought and ran a shop as a witness, he was finally accepted at Moorlands Bible College in 1988.

Clearly, it was at Moorlands that Simon and Sharon met and as their relationship developed, so their mutual interest and desire to serve in mission came into focus. As both of them had served in rural area they thought that that would be where they ended up.

During her time at college, Sharon had a number of illnesses that left her wondering exactly what would happen – meningitis, viral pneumonia, pleurisy and TB (this had lay dormant since her time in Africa). Simon had bought a book for 50p, written by Viv Grigg called 'Companion to the Poor' about his work with the urban poor in Manila. Simon was greatly affected reading this book, but Sharon refused to read it until she was in an isolation ward recovering from the TB. When she did so, she, too, realised that this was the area that God was calling them to work in.

They were married in July 1990 and after graduating a year later joined Worldwide Evangelisation for Christ (better known as WEC International). WEC have an intense programme of training before acceptance – it is a four month candidate's course during which no decision is made until the very end at an intimidating meeting in which everyone involved is present and able to speak out and decide whether candidates are accepted or otherwise.

After that intense period, Simon and Sharon were finally accepted as WEC missionaries. Whilst at Bulstrode (WEC headquarters), they had learnt that that there was a work starting in Mexico City and the opportunity to work with the urban poor in shanty towns. Firstly they went to Costa Rica to learn Spanish.

During her final months at college and at Bulstrode, Sharon suffered from 'blackouts' which at first the doctors thought were mini-strokes, then they thought the problem was epilepsy and so coupled with the other illnesses Sharon had been very ill for around five years. Finally they diagnosed an on-going gynaecological problem, which was not finally solved until a hysterectomy that Sharon underwent when she and Simon were in Costa Rica.

These chronic illnesses understandably affected Simon and Sharon's resolve to a degree. How were they ever going to survive in a foreign land without the medical facilities that they had experienced in England? For Simon the resolution was easier. He felt the call to mission at the age of 19; after his time in Kenya he had at first been rejected by Moorlands, but kept on trying and eventually was accepted. Even while they were at WEC, initially they were turned down at the end of the four months, but then this decision was reversed. Sharon's illness had delayed their move to Costa Rica and then Mexico by another year. It had taken 10 years before Simon finally got onto the mission field and he had had to overcome many hurdles – from his experience his advice is do not give up, keep on trying and the door will open.

Sharon's reassurance came through a different way. Before they were to travel to Costa Rica, she underwent a quick operation in order to make things alright for them to travel, the doctors however found further problems and this meant more delay. It was during this time that Sharon was reading through Hebrews, when a particular passage came to mean so much to her:

> So do not throw away your confidence; it will be richly rewarded. You need to persevere so that when you have done the will of God, you will receive what He has promised. For in a little while, 'He who is coming will come and will not delay. But my righteous one will live by faith. And if he shrinks back I will not be pleased with him' (Hebrews 10:35-38, with a quotation from Habakkuk 2:3-4).

She was determined to see through the calling that she had received, even through some more difficult times as the necessity for that final operation in Costa Rica occurred.

Of course, even after that operation, it did not mean that were not more hurdles to face. Simon and particularly Sharon had to come to terms with the fact that they would not be able to have children and Sharon had gone through an operation that causes many women who go through the same procedure much trauma; even more testing was that Sharon was far away from the support of friends and family.

In the meantime they were preparing for the work in Mexico. Simon picked up the language quickly and within the year was preaching in Spanish and at one stage even interpreted for an Irishman who was in court in Costa Rica! Sharon, understandably, found the language harder to pick up but kept on battling. They also began to work with street kids there as well.

Finally, in April 1994, they arrived in Mexico only to discover that the Field Leader of WEC there tried to persuade them not to work in Mexico City, but to join the rest of the team a little way away and not working in an urban setting. Needless to say after all that they had been through, Simon and Sharon were not going to be stopped at that late stage.

For three years they worked with a local Pastor helping to plant a church in one of the shanty towns. They ran Sunday Schools, youth work, Bible studies, holiday Bible clubs – they did receive help from short term teams from time to time – they also taught English locally in order to build up contacts. Much of their time was spent building relationships – for example they met each week with a family whose daughter had cerebral palsy, who would normally have been rejected by even her own society. They became well known in the local shanty towns as they were the only foreigners in the vicinity and after those three years they felt that they 'belonged'.

During that time they also looked at the possibility of adopting a child in Mexico; they had no intention of leaving the country and naturally wanted a family. After a number of false alarms, they were finally able to adopt a young girl, called Ruth. It was not without many, many difficulties and did at times distract from the work at hand, but missionaries are human too. In may ways adopting a baby and all of the problems that they went through, helped to build further relationships, as it showed their vulnerability and to the locals it was hard to understand why a 'white couple' would want a Mexican baby!

At the end of three years, they went home on furlough and had received a positive evaluation from the Field Leader. However after being in England for one month, they received a letter from him telling them not to return. Naturally they were confused and heartbroken. The local office tried to intervene but to no avail. He was adamant that they should not continue their work in the shanty towns. With the way WEC operates each Field Leader is autonomous and can make such decisions without reference to an International Office.

For a year they tried to get the Leader in Mexico to reconsider, but it was not to be. The Pastor in Mexico even suggested that they return independently to continue the work but they were so shattered by the events that they were in no fit state to carry on the work.

In 1998, they officially left WEC and came to Northern Ireland, homeless and broken. Simon got a job as a book-keeper with Corrymeela in Belfast and Sharon started to work with Christians Providing Care in Ballybeen Estate in Dundonald. It took them two years before they could even consider mission again. By that time they had settled in Newtownards and were attending Ards Evangelical Church. They have also adopted another child, Richard.

Even after all that they had been through, once you have got the mission 'bug' it is hard to settle fully back into everyday life. Both Sharon and Simon have both found it hard to cope with the 'Western' world again. In February 2001, Simon left Corrymeela and stepped out in faith to represent People International (P.I.) in Ireland. P.I. work in the Muslim world along the 'Silk Road'; they have had no previous 'presence' in the Province and so Simon has been working from scratch trying to build up contacts and visiting churches. It has been difficult but he has built up good working relationships with the other mission representatives and together they work to inform and educate about mission.

Their original call was to work in a cross-cultural ministry and they have been praying for some time about the need to get back involved more directly. Simon and Sharon recently applied to Operation Mobilisation to join one of the ships, but there are no spaces at the moment for a family of four and so that is a further set back for them: however, they continue to actively seek God's will and other opportunities. They have the support of their leaders at Ards Evangelical and, despite all of their setbacks, heartbreaks and difficulties they are determined to fulfil their call.

Their steadfastness in the midst of all the problems is a salutary lesson to us all; particularly if we are tempted to give up at the first hurdle. Pray for them and if God is speaking to you – do not give up, persevere as the writer to the Hebrews commented: 'we are not of those who shrink back...but of those who believe (Hebrews 10:39).

## SPIRITUAL SIGHT
Robert Lacey

There is nothing that can stop God from fulfilling his purposes and no Christian is outside of His plan. Your background and history can be hindering factors but cannot prevent God working; sickness can hinder but will not stop the Lord. On conversion we become new creations and God wants to use us all. Robert Lacey has a deteriorating eye condition that means he cannot drive and his eyesight is poor – but that does not stop him being involved in the way that God wants. It is mentioned now because in many ways it is not relevant to the rest of his testimony.

Robert was not brought up in a Christian home but has no particular wish that things were different. "I saw what it was like to grow up in a home where drink often had an influence" he says and that helps him to relate to many of the children that he has worked with over the years. He became a Christian in 1970 as a teenager just after his sister. Then his mother became a Christian soon afterwards. They waited another 12 years before his father surrendered his life to Christ.

He got married in 1975 to Irene and attended Abbots Cross Congregational. Robert continued to work in mechanical engineering and Irene as a nurse, which they both thoroughly enjoyed. As they continued to grow, they for around three years met together for fellowship and sharing with a group of around twenty people. This proved to be spiritual training ground and out of those twenty around a dozen are now in full time Christian work,

Robert says that he and Irene "quietly felt that the Lord had something for them" but struggled with the whole concept of "a call". He spoke to his minister, Rev. Shaw, about this area. Is it enough just to see the need? Rev. Shaw advised that he should not move until he saw something from God's Word. At that time they supported the work of CEF and were attending conferences and other meetings. It was at one of the Easter Conferences that Robert was approached to consider joining the work. As they prayed and considered this, a verse came into Robert's mind for which he did not know the reference 'I will instruct you and teach you'. As he continued his regular Bible readings he came to Psalm 32, which is exactly where the verse is found and since has become a particular significant passage. The full verse (8) reads:

I will instruct you and teach you in the way you should go;

I will counsel you and watch over you.

Inevitably questions come when a decision is made to leave secure, paid employment to 'live by faith'. What would happen if they left their jobs and it proved to be the wrong move? They would be left with egg on their faces, as it were, and would feel extremely foolish. Robert and Irene were ready to be wrong. They trusted the Lord. For Robert and Irene it is enough that God knows.

They went to Bible college for one year and then to the CEF training school in Switzerland for three months before embarking on the work in the Co. Antrim area. He is now the local Director for CEF with his main role being to enthuse and involve others in evangelism. He still takes opportunities for direct evangelism, but most of his time is spent training and motivating others to get involved.

There are a number of courses that are available through CEF that help prepare for children's evangelism. Currently there is a sixteen week course which aims to share how to teach children effectively. There are levels each looking at different aspects of children's work; level two for example develops the skills to encourage children to grow spiritually. One thing that Robert has learned over the years is that often there can be effective evangelism, which results in responses from the children, but some, because of their location or backgrounds can be left in a kind of vacuum. The Christian life does not stop at conversion and spiritual growth must be maintained throughout a child's development.

Robert's dedication to the work of reaching children with the gospel and discipling those who respond to the gospel message is clear and is matched by his wife who has been a partner in the work from the outset. There are often events in your life that make an impact that stay with you. One such in Robert's life is working with John Drane, as a young man years before he joined CEF. As they prayed for the children they were reaching, John would weep for the children. This was the first time that Robert had ever come across anyone weeping for the souls of the lost – it has clearly influenced Robert's attitude towards the children that he and the others that he works with reach through the work of CEF.

When Robert was growing up, before he and his family had become Christians, there was a family joke that the black sheep of the family was a relation who was a Presbyterian Minister – the only 'good living' one among them. How things have changed through the grace of the Lord Jesus, because it is not just Robert who is involved in missionary work – his sister works with New Tribes Mission.

## NOT YET FINISHED
Violet McCombe


It is clear that Violet trusts God; right from her conversion at the age of 10 she has been aware that God has a plan for her life. She asks the question: 'Are all God's objectives perfectly reached?' In response Violet believes that God does make allowances, but 'that through His patience, grace and mercy He does ultimately achieve His goal – that is to conform those who are His to the image of His Son'. Violet believes that we all should be aware of the plan of God as, for example, Paul writes to the Ephesians that they had been chosen in Him (Jesus) before the creation of the world to be holy and blameless in His sight (Ephesians 1: 4) and David knew that God had recorded His daily objectives for his life even before he was formed in his mother's womb (see Psalm 139:16).

Violet has been serving the Lord in Africa and the Middle East since 1968 and she has been through many different experiences that have not shaken her trust in God. Her interest in missions was stirred by an aunt who was a missionary, who later became a faithful prayer supporter for Violet. It was increased by her elder sister who developed a great interest in missions. But all of that would count for nothing unless Violet herself responded to God's call on her life.

She trained as a General Nurse and then moved into the more specialised area of midwifery. She was conscious of her need to develop her skills and after much prayer and consideration she went to the Faith Mission Bible College. One of the more practical considerations was that of developing the ability of speaking in public, which Violet knew would be difficult for her, but she also knew that she would be 'in at the deep end' at the Faith Mission, where there is a great practical emphasis on public speaking and preaching.

The Bible is a book that is God's living Word to Violet and throughout her life she has been reassured through verses and God speaking through Scripture. Before going to Bible College for example, Psalm 32:8 'I will instruct you and teach you in the way you should go, and I will guide you with my eye' was particularly significant and has remained a verse that has comforted Violet through all of her journeys. Violet also sensed her need of empowering of the Holy Spirit in readiness for her service and journey into the unknown. The 1960s was a time when there was a renewing move of the ministry of the Holy Spirit in churches and Violet sought the filling and empowering of the Holy Spirit in fresh way to challenge and make her ready for service. Violet identifies with the thought of Catherine Marshall, who wrote of our need not to put any stumbling block in the way of the 'housekeeping' of the Holy Spirit, where he refurbishes and refreshes. As Violet says, 'The dust can so easily gather in my life which leads to spiritual lethargy. I need the "Divine Housekeeper!"'

Violet arrived in Eritrea in October 1968. Recently she met a missionary, who had five children, who told her, 'I was just one year old when you went to Eritrea!' This caused Violet to reflect on what she had done in those 35 years. As she did so she realised the more important question was, 'What had God done in her?' As she considered this, whilst recognising the difficulty of assessing our own progress, she wonders whether there really have been any steps forward, with all the lessons she has had to learn and sometimes re-learn. One presumes that others who have worked and served with Violet would have a different perspective.

Throughout the nine years that Violet was there, she experienced the help and guidance of the Lord, particularly in one instance, when, as the surgeon could not return to the hospital in time, she and others performed an emergency operation in order to save lives. Eritrea was suffering from a civil war for all those years and the situation just got worse and worse. All aspects of life were affected particularly travel as well as being caught in the middle of the two opposing sides.

In 1977 the situation got critical and Violet was caught up in the Liberation Front's assault on Tesseni in Eritrea. The attack became known as the '4, 4, 4 Battle' since it started at 4am on the 4th day of the 4th month. As Violet was at church that first day, in the midst of the raging battle of machines guns and fighter jets, so the Lord gave her another verse from the Psalms – 'I shall not die but live, and will proclaim what the Lord has done' (Psalm 118:7) – which proved to be an encouragement then and true personally when after eight days of trying to treat the wounded with few resources Violet and a colleague escaped across the Sudan border to safety.

During the time that Violet had been in Eritrea, the missionary organisation had merged with two Middle East Missions, which enabled Violet to move into a new area of study, that of Arabic language. After she had completed that study, Violet wanted to go and use the skills picked up, but the leadership of the mission wanted her to return to East Sudan, because of her previous experiences, to work with Eritrean refugees. Violet admits that not being able to build on the Arabic immediately left some regret, but over the years she learnt that she could trust the Lord in all things and that in His time, His purposes are fulfilled. It was more important then that the Lord worked in and through Violet rather than her becoming fluent in Arabic.

She did have other opportunities to work in Arab countries. She particularly appreciated the opportunity to work in a small maternity hospital in the Arab Emirates, for a year, as not only did she work in 'proper' conditions but also experienced spiritual fellowship that was lacking in the Sudan.

Later in 1991, whilst doing a short literary Arabic course, Violet briefly joined a small medical team in the west of Iran in order to help the Iraqi Kurds who had come over the mountains after the

Gulf War. There Violet was deeply moved by the many sacrifices that Iranian church members made so they could serve and help the refugees. One Christian man who served in the camp was later to be martyred for his faith. It was this man's wife who had had a dream where she saw the Lord standing in line with the Kurdish people, in Kurdish dress, waiting for food – it was a powerful reminder to all those there that the service to the Kurds was a service to him and that is true of all of our true service. In the Middle East where there has yet to be great reaping of souls, it is reassuring to all those who work there that nothing that the Lord gives to do and nothing that is done for Him is ever wasted.

Whilst working in the Sudan, Violet realised that she was treating children for diseases that were, for the most part, preventable and so she developed a Health Education programme as 'prevention is (always) better than cure'. She began a series of Community Health programmes in Sudanese villages which sought to reduce the number of children, in particular, from becoming sick in the first place. She ran these from 1986-1988 and 1992-1994. After that she worked for seven years working for the International Office of Middle East Christian Outreach on behalf of the Mission's personnel. However, she never lost the desire to use her Arabic language skill along with her Community Health programme and so in 2002, she went to the country in which she had that original desire to serve way back in 1978 after her initial language training. It took 14 years but now she teaches basic health care to 'health teams' in villages in the beautiful mountains and valleys, so that they can return to their villages and train the villagers. Her desire to see the light of the gospel penetrate and change darkened hearts has never wavered, and she trusts that through what she does, the Lord will speak into those lives.

Violet is now experiencing that God really does work out everything for the good of those who love Him and are called according to His purpose. She did not know it then but the Lord had a reason for not fulfilling her desires in 1978 and all that she has experienced in the intervening years have been a training ground for her current work.

Like the valleys and mountains in which she works, the service of Violet McCombe has been through the valleys and in the mountain places; there have difficulties, dangers and hard lessons to learn – which does go to show that missionaries are ordinary Christians, they struggle like the rest and do not have all of the answers – but after over 25 years of service, Violet is not finished. Why? Because the Lord has not finished with her yet – as Violet herself says, 'The Potter is still working on the clay. It's clay that needs much working.'

Violet McCombe is not finished – it is time that some of us started!

## THE DUNKIRK SPIRIT
(That is, reaching into Dunkirk, not leaving!)
Alan and Valerie Kyle

Throughout the history of Christian mission over the last 200 years, one group of Christians have sent more workers to the mission field, in proportion to their total membership, than any other Christian group – they are the Christian Brethren. Without any formal denominational structure, the workers have gone out to various parts of the world but particularly to Africa and South and Central America.

In its earliest and probably truest form, the Christians who became known as the 'Brethren' wanted to move away from the 'high' church trappings and move back to what they considered the simple meetings of the Early Church of the New Testament times. Originally meeting to remember the Lord at 'the Lord's Table' (communion), they had a high regard for the Word of God and the command of the Lord to go into all the world to preach the gospel. Many responded and living by faith, they stepped out to serve the Lord where they felt He called.

Whilst many things may have changed from the early days of George Mueller and his contemporaries, there is still an emphasis on mission. Alan, from Northamptonshire, and Valerie, from Dundonald, were both brought up at local Gospel Halls. Alan's parents were both Christians who were committed members of the local assembly (as Brethren churches prefer to be known). He became a Christian at a children's mission held by a local Evangelist, Ivor Powell in 1967 at the age of 12 and was baptised four years later.

Valerie's mother was a Christian but her father was not. However, she attended Dundonald Gospel Hall and became a Christian after a baptismal service at the church. At that time Dundonald Gospel Hall had a vibrant youth group and Valerie was greatly influenced by Drew Craig, a Bible teacher through whom Valerie developed a great love for God's Word.

Alan and Valerie did not meet in England nor in Northern Ireland, but in France in 1997, when both were part of the Gospel Literature Outreach (GLO) team that was working in Caen in Normandy. For Valerie this was all part and parcel of an interest in France and all things French that had been developing since the age of 11. Alan had already been to Caen with GLO in 1975, which had helped to kindle his interest in the country. Valerie had also visited France with another organisation called Young Pioneers.

Alan and Valerie both recognise the part that visiting missionaries and missionary conferences had in helping them to develop an interest in missions. Valerie felt the first call of God when she was listening to a French missionary, Leonore Souza, at a ladies meeting at her home assembly. At first she was overwhelmed by the need, but slowly she realised that she could do a small part, realising that God does not want us to solve every problem, instead to do what He calls us to do.

Their separate desire to serve the Lord in France was confirmed by keeping in touch with missionaries as well as maintaining a close study of Scripture and was aided when they met each other. They had to wait some time before the time was right. Alan for seven years before he left his 'secure' employment in the bank to move onto the mission field with Valerie and their 11 month old baby. For Valerie she waited for 10 years before she went to live in France; but those years were not wasted years, God was using them as a training ground preparing them for the work that was ahead. France was always going to be the place where they were to serve

- as they say: "Although we were aware of the needs elsewhere, we never felt called to another country. God placed in our hearts a love and true compassion for France. Our missionary friends were in France, we went on outreach teams to France every year and we met in France!"

At first they worked with a local church in Rambouillet, near Paris, which is a pleasant commuter town of around 27,000 people. When they arrived the church had only four members and their role was obviously to help the church to grow, by God's grace. For seventeen years they undertook various forms of evangelism and the church grew steadily, rather than dramatically, but had reached 50 members by the time they had left – at its peak the numbers had reached 70. After 17 years they felt that they had given all they could to the fellowship and that it was time to move on; this would also give a fresh start to the local believers too.

After much prayer and seeking God's will as well as taking advice from other Christians, they moved to Dunkirk. It was important that the Kyles were sure of what God was wanting them to do as any move meant a change of school for their three sons as well as the impact on the church they were leaving behind as well as the new one.

Since 1999, they have been working with the fellowship there in Dunkirk, which has around 225,000 inhabitants. Dunkirk is completely different from Rambouillet as it is more working class and has many social problems. The local church was also in serious trouble with falling membership and much difficulty among the fellowship. At the time closing the church was a distinct possibility. Alan and Valerie have the mission to get the church back on the rails and for it to be an effective witness for Christ.

The work is demanding and difficult, but much progress has been made and over the last four and a half years the membership has quadrupled, with the work amongst young people having a great impact. Alan and Valerie are also involved in the expanding work of the Dunkirk Christian Bookshop. They do feel as they look back that the move they made was right as the Lord has blessed all richly, including the church back in Rambouillet.

Alan and Valerie understand that the time will come when their work will come to an end at Dunkirk too, since it is part of their desire to hand the leadership over to indigenous French full-time workers. In the meantime they have no plans to return to the UK. Their wish is to fulfil the call of God and to see the work in Dunkirk continue to grow and thrive, according to God's grace and mercy.

France is a secular society and that permeates every area of life – whilst religious education is banned in school, the children are given an atheistic flavour and so this needs to be combated by an effective and secure family life as well as a good church life. Life as a Christian worker is never easy, even in a developed country like France. Alan and Valerie recommend that anyone considering mission work should be sure of God's call because as times get hard, particularly in the early years the devil will always be telling you to give up.

Although as prepared as you feel, nothing will ever fully prepare you for the difficulties and the experiences you will face, so a close daily walk with the Lord is vital. Despite all of the difficulties that they have faced over the years such as disputes in the church, the hard soil in terms of evangelism, settling into a different culture and so on, Alan and Valerie believe that their life has been a great adventure of trusting God, especially when they have run out of solutions and they have had to look on as God has worked His purposes out. Nothing can replace the joy of seeing people, whose lives are wrecked by sin, transformed by the power of the gospel.

I suspect that many of us have felt a 'twinge' as we have listened to missionaries in the past; perhaps we have ignored that feeling that God is calling us because we are too overwhelmed by the work or because we are too afraid. The call for the labourers is still there. France, like many European countries, has a great need for help in the work of the gospel and in establishing churches. Do not be afraid if God is calling – trust Him, test the waters as it were and get involved – as Alan and Valerie say: "Not only are there opportunities in France...we desperately need more help in Dunkirk!"

In the words of the man of Macedonia: 'Come over and help us!'

## NOT FLORENCE NIGHTINGALE
(but in the Crimea)
Emma Cousley


So what do you know about the Crimea? There was a war in the late 1800s, where Florence Nightingale first came to fame. Did you know that it's in the Ukraine? Did you know that the International Federation of Evangelical Students (IFES) has a worker from Northern Ireland there?

Emma Cousley was brought up in a Christian home and became a Christian at a Scripture Union (SU) in 1990, when she was 12. As she progressed through her teenage years, she matured as a Christian and attended Scripture Union, youth fellowships and Bible classes and a desire to love and serve God also grew. However, like many, she struggled with a constant walk, found it difficult to read her Bible and pray regularly and felt that she could never live up to the expectations of how Christians should live.

After being accepted into the University of Ulster at Jordanstown, she soon got involved in the Christian Union, became part of a small group Bible study and made friends on her course. But she was very unhappy. She was finding it difficult to see how God was working in her life. After much prayer made on her behalf, she was accepted onto a teacher training course at Stranmillis College in Belfast. Emma had never really had a great desire to be a teacher, nevertheless it was all part of the Lord's plan for her.

She soon settled in at Stranmillis, joining the Christian Union and a small group Bible study, later that year Emma was elected onto the leadership committee of the CU and started to work closely with the IFES staff worker at the college. Around that time the then IFES Ireland executive director, Cassells Morrell (now Director of the IFES work across Western Europe) spoke at the CU houseparty and what he had to say had a great impact on Emma. He spoke frankly and honestly about his own sin, which Emma had never heard anyone do before, especially someone in Christian leadership. It came as great relief to her to realise that everyone was in the same boat as herself, constantly struggling with imperfection.

It was at Stranmillis that Emma had her most significant time of spiritual growth; being part of the CU leadership, discipling fellow students, attending conferences on student leadership and how to study the Bible, going on IFES summer evangelism teams all contributed to her realisation that although she was a bigger sinner than she could ever imagine, God is far greater and His grace extends to beyond all that she could ever imagine. As a forgiven child of God, He has made her righteous and perfect in Christ and He delights in her. She came to understand that God has chosen to use weak and sinful people to bring about His purposes. (All of which is true for every Christian!) Emma truly experienced the grace of God in her life during this time, which brought healing and the freedom to serve God.

The IFES staff worker and other staff of IFES Ireland made a great impact on Emma's life, through their own lives and service and so when Emma graduated she had come to realise the strategic role that students had to play in the spread of the gospel and she had a desire to pass on to other students what she had learnt and experienced that she spent a year as part of the UCCF (University and Colleges Christian Fellowship) RELAY team, a discipleship training programme for recent graduates, working alongside the staff worker at Stranmillis and Jordanstown, supporting and discipling the CU leaders.

Interestingly, Emma had felt that once she completed her teacher training that if she did not have specific call to stay and teach in Northern Ireland, then she should go somewhere else[1]. It was not surprising then that she felt at home with IFES, with their like passion for students and the impact that IFES had had on her own life. A number of factors have led her to the Ukraine, experience of friends, the climate and that IFES Ireland has an established link with IFES in the Ukraine.

So Emma has ended up working in the Crimea with international students for two years, basically undertaking a staffworker role, assisting the local workers in the University. She leads Bible studies with Malaysian students who are based at the University in Simferopol in the Crimea. Emma obviously encounters some language difficulties, but is able to work alongside those who speak English. As a stranger in a strange land she is able to empathise with much of what the students are going through. The Ukraine is an expanding area of work for IFES and has recently established a National Office, with a local board of directors. It has a staff team of 26, with three-quarters coming from the Ukraine and the rest being international staff from the USA, Canada and Norway (and Emma!) CCX (as IFES is known in the Ukraine, Russia and Belarus) works in 14 universities across the vast country and since 1990 has been involved with over 2000 students. Being such a large country, Emma and the team in the Crimea are some way away from the office in Kiev.

So what is it like to go to a foreign country and try to serve the Lord? Emma's experiences are not untypical. On the second day she wept as she tried to overcome the overwhelming feelings of loneliness, what lies ahead and the daunting task of learning a new language. As she cried and cried out to God, the reassurance of His presence, His goodness, His faithfulness and that He knew best emerged from the tears.

The first few months were spent in language study and orientation, then she had to readjust again as she moved to Simferopol. Initially, the intention was that she was to work with

---

[1] It was Keith Green in the 1980s, before he died in a tragic air crash with three of his young children, who passionately put forward this concept that as Jesus has already commanded us to go (Matthew 28:19,20), it should be the exception if we stay.

Ukrainian students and to support the work already going on. However, on discovering a significant group of Christian Malaysian students at the Medical University, she developed contacts and attended a student church where many of them went and found an American couple who also wanted to develop the work with these foreign students. They meet with around 40 students in weekly Bible studies and are developing discipleship through various other ventures.

In many ways the work that Emma is involved in is a departure from the 'usual' IFES work, in that she is working with foreign as opposed to national students. What happens after Emma returns to Northern Ireland is unclear (will the local office continue the work with foreign students?); nevertheless, the blessing that Emma has been is unquestioned and God has been working in and through these Malaysian students in their growth and discipleship.

Emma's experiences once more show how God chooses to use ordinary people to serve Him in a variety of ways. Sometimes it can be difficult at first, but God is faithful and His purposes are worked out. Is the Lord speaking to you about more service at home or abroad? Don't resist but trust Him completely.

## EXPLORE, DREAM, DISCOVER
Ian and Claire Gray

It was way back in 1964 that Ian and Claire Gray first took the step to go to the mission field and 40 years later, they are still going strong. As they look back, they realise not just how much society has changed in those years, but also Christian attitudes towards service. When they first went, they knew and imagined that their missionary service would be for life; today far more service is done on a short-term basis.

The trouble is the sort of work that the Grays have been involved in cannot really be done in a couple of years...but more of that later. Once again God has been pleased to bring together a Northern Irish lady and an Englishman to work together in His plans, (see also the Kyles and the Carters).

Claire was brought up in a solid Christian home attending Monkstown Baptist Church and became a Christian at 11 years old. A couple of years later she remembers being distinctly challenged and a desire to work overseas was triggered at the tender age of 13, not as a nurse, she determined, but as a teacher.

And that is exactly what happened; after leaving school, she trained to be teacher and worked for five years at Woodburn School. By that time she had also met Ian after a summer outreach in Millisle. During the outreach, she had come across a number of children from disadvantaged backgrounds from Belfast and after the summer continued with the contact and went along to Donegal Square Methodist Church, which is where she met Ian.

Ian had not been brought up in a Christian home, but had become a Christian after reading through the gospel of John and in particular, chapter 14. He was studying Hebrew and Greek with a view to become a Methodist minister. He met an old Methodist minister who had been a missionary in Nigeria and had translated the Bible into the Engone language and had mentioned to Ian about 'a group of people known as Wycliffe Bible Translators, who are very professional'. This set Ian's mind thinking about the possibility of using his skills and abilities in Bible translation. Soon afterwards he was waiting for Claire in Belfast and the bus stop was outside Erskine Mayne bookshop. In the window he saw the display of the book called '2000 Tongues to go: the Story of Wycliffe Bible Translators'. Never having heard of them before, Ian clearly felt the call of God on his life.

The truth is that God was calling both of them independently to serve him overseas and so when they told each other of how God was speaking to them, each was overjoyed to discover that God had been leading them. They were married in 1962 and then in 1964 were accepted into Wycliffe. Another change over the years is the way that mission organisations deal with candidates for the mission field; these days there are often many hurdles to climb over and hoops to clamber trough prior to acceptance, in the 1960s it was a little easier but nevertheless, because of the life commitment that it involved was an enormous step to take.

After a year in Bible College in France, Ian and Claire set out with a seven month old son, Clive, to travel to Nigeria to work with the Enugu people in September 1965. At that time, missionaries were told where to go, as it were, and although their original desire was to go and work with a specific and new language group, they were placed in a team ministry, where each couple took turns at looking after the needs of the other field missionaries and developing the service of hospitality. Not exactly where they would have chosen but a good training ground.

In June 1967, the Biafrian war caused them to be evacuated and they went to Ghana to work with the Tampulma people group. The Tampulma people live across a river, which restricts movement as the only way across is by canoe and during the rainy season the area is almost completely cut off.

Ian and Claire then set to work to translate the Bible into the local language. First of all they had to learn the language, which had never been written down before – only spoken. They learnt phonetically and eventually formed an alphabet. To them the grammar is a pattern that has to be worked out.

Once the alphabet had been composed, so Ian could set to work on the actual translation of the New Testament and Claire taught the people to read, using Bible stories. As they lived among the people over the years, they learned to think like the people and started to understand the dos and the don'ts. For example, the men had to be taught first, before the women. Now many of those first men are leaders and pastors in the churches.

Ten years after they first arrived in Tampulma, the New Testament was completed and a couple of years after that, Ian and Claire returned with their growing family to represent Wycliffe in Northern Ireland from 1979-1984. The Tampulna people however were now requesting that the Old Testament be translated so that they had the whole Bible.

Over the last ten years, then, the Grays have been sharing their time between Ghana and Northern Ireland and Ian had translated the whole Bible into the Tampulna language by the year 2000. However, Claire in particular has developed another part to her service in that she was asked to go over to France to help with refugees and began a work with displaced people from Cambodia and so each summer Claire and a team go to France.

Time has moved on for the Grays; their children have all grown up and are also dedicated to serving the Lord in various ways and in different places and the Grays are not yet ready to hang up their missionary boots just yet either. They have inspired many to consider service for the Lord and their dedication, like that of Mary Steele, stands out in these days of short-term contracts. Claire is committed to writing regularly to all their supporters and friends, motivating and encouraging. Ian continues to give service in translation. The Bible has now been translated into 5000 different dialects in Africa and there are still 100 left to go.

Ghana and the Tampulna people have also moved on since 1967. Seventy-five percent of the people are now literate and the projects that are being undertaken are seeking to provide means whereby the people themselves can sustain the on-going work. A clinic and a new school have been built, but the question was asked, 'how are these going to keep going?' The answer was to provide 47 cows so that the people can provide for their own needs. There is a high percentage of Christians among the Tampulna people and so they are determined to succeed.

Mark Twain wrote:

> Twenty years from now you will be more disappointed by the things you didn't do than by the ones you did do, so throw off the bow lines. Sail away from the safe harbour. Catch the trade winds in your sails. Explore, Dream, Discover.

Ian and Claire Gray after 40 years have explored, dreamed and discovered. The Bible in the Tampulna language is testimony to that; the number of Christians in the area also bear witness to that; the many people that have been touched by their lives in Northern Ireland, Africa and even France echo the fact loud and clear. They continue to serve the Lord and encourage many others to do the same. As we all reflect on what has gone before and anticipate what lies ahead will we remain safely in the harbour, with a life of regrets of what we did not do? Or are we ready to throw off our bow lines and step out for the Lord? Let us explore, dream and discover the great things that the Lord has planned for us!

## ONCE NOT TWICE
John and Leena Brown

"No-one has the right to hear the gospel twice until
everyone has heard it once."
(Oswald J Smith 'The Challenge of Mission',
originally published as 'The Cry of the World')

John Brown first read this in a borrowed library book and it made a
great impact on him then and still does today. John did not grow up
in a Christian home, but was converted at the age of seven. His next
door neighbours were Christians and they used to hold children's
meetings in their garage and through this work and going along to
church John was converted.

Mr and Mrs Wright, the neighbours, had been missionaries
and so all of the children were exposed to mission work right from
the start. The grounding that John got in his formative years was
vital – Mrs Wright ran a Bible club and John was good friends with
their son Chris.

John was an avid reader of missionary biographies and
visited the local library regularly to borrow books on mission, which
is where he first picked up the Oswald Smith book. As he read he
was challenged as to why it is that many hear the gospel over and

over again whilst millions have yet to hear. He believes, looking back, that it was then he had the stirrings of a call to mission work, but it did not blossom for many years.

As we grow up through our teenage years often our focus begins to change; passing exams, getting a job and even getting involved in local church life can all affect how we view the world and the work of mission. John was no different – it wasn't that he entered a life of crime or started drinking binges or any type of backslidden behaviour, but rather that he just got involved in what he was doing without thinking about missions.

That was all to change in the summer of 1972; by that time John had studied at Lisburn Tech. and had begun working as a Consulting Engineer. However a summer campaign with Operation Mobilisation led him to a significant crossroads. The call to mission had returned and decisions had to be made. OM wanted John to go to India – but that was not in his plans! He thought that he would have to go to Bible College, but that was not a favoured option either. This was all made the more difficult by the fact that his family were not all that supportive; in particular his father was extremely sceptical.

It seems that joining a mission organisation thirty years ago was a lot simpler than it is now – John handed in his notice when he returned from the summer programme, joined OM in September and, after a period of orientation, arrived in India in October!

From Northern Ireland to India – John certainly found the whole experience, once he had arrived as a tremendous eye-opener. There were just masses of people everywhere and what is more they were fighting to get hold of tracts! The Indians actually wanted to buy literature and books and they really enjoyed talking about God!

Every day John would go to bed thoroughly exhausted after organising open air meetings that would reach thousands of people, who had never heard about Jesus before, with the gospel. These first few years were immensely satisfying and motivating and still remain for John some of the best years that he has ever experienced.

After a couple of years John was appointed to one other person to undertake Bible teaching across the land. They taught for 10 days and moved from centre to centre. This entailed being trained and putting together a series of teaching programmes so for John this filled the void of not having been to Bible College; except it was an extremely practical course.

As has been mentioned before, John looks back very fondly on his 12 years in India. OM had, and still has, a vision to reach everybody in India with the gospel. In 1972 the population was 550 million, now it is 1 billion – the population has doubled in thirty years! All of the hard work that was put in those early years has, over the last decade, being paying dividends. For John and his team most of their work was sowing, laying and preparing the ground for the reaping that took place in the nineties.

Many of the early converts are now leaders in India today and that is all part of God's timing and plan. In the seventies, foreigners were treated with respect and their message listened to, nowadays however, it is much more beneficial for the nationals themselves to be mainly involved in the evangelism.

Another reason why John enjoyed his time in India is that it was while he was there that he met and married (in 1976) Leena, who had come to India with OM from Finland. All three of their children were also born in India.

In 1983, John was heavily involved in the organising of the Ganges Outreach '83, part of the all India programme, where a state or area would be saturated, as it were, for 3 months. During this time there was much activity in the Bihar State and this in turn caused visa problems for the Browns – in effect John became a 'persona non grata'.

After 12 years, working mainly amongst Hindus, John and Leena began to pray about what was next for them. It became clear that they were being led towards the Muslim world; in the meantime they were invited to join the Doulos ship as leaders in charge of training and evangelism for two years as it travelled in Europe and Africa. This they agreed to, but they knew that this move would not be 'for ever' and that their hearts lay elsewhere.

In 1986, John, Leena and family were invited to go to Pakistan. Opportunities were expanding in Pakistan and in many ways it was in a similar situation to that of India in the early seventies. John took on the responsibility of Field Leadership in Pakistan, responsible for 50 or 60 people, discipling, encouraging, motivating, training and preparing future leaders amongst the nationals.

After five years in 1991, the time was right to move on – the nationals were now in a position to take on the field leadership and there were also family considerations to bear in mind. The children were in need of secondary education and also of some form of identity. They had been born in India to a Northern Irish father and a Finnish mother, had moved from place to place on the Doulos and spent five years in Pakistan – who were they?

On top of this after nearly twenty years on the mission field John and Leena were 'burnt out' and in many ways just wanted to be 'normal' again. After they left Pakistan they came to Northern Ireland. The settling in period took longer than they anticipated – the children probably adapted more quickly than John and Leena as John admits, "It took us four years to feel at home."

Time had moved on and John could not get back into the building trade. Leena had trained as a nurse in Finland, but her qualifications were not recognised in the U.K. and so a period of re-training had to take place. John took up painting and decorating and ran his own small business, but there was no real satisfaction.

They had maintained their links with OM as John had joined the local OM council and in 1995, the local representative post became vacant and John took on the role. Now his responsibilities involved encouraging interest, recruiting short term and longer term workers, keeping prayer partners and supporters informed and planning itineraries of visiting speakers.

Over the years there has been a shift in how churches view mission. In the past, mission was done by missionaries with churches sending money. Now many churches want to be far more involved. The missionaries are seen as representatives of the church and there is a heightened sense of responsibility to keep them informed. The churches have become much more active partners.

It is now thirteen years since the Browns returned to Northern Ireland, the children are now all grown up and have left home – each following the Lord – and John and Leena have settled into their lives serving the Lord in representing the work of OM. However John says, "There comes a point when you ask yourself – 'Why am I asking others to go, when I can go myself?'"

John and Leena have a few years left of active service and they have always felt the call to work in a cross-cultural setting, reaching the unreached and so over the last couple of years have been asking the Lord to show them whether it was time for them to move on. Another crossroad was reached on 6th March 2003, when they made the decision that God was calling them to move into another area of pioneering work. In seeking their children's reaction, particularly their youngest daughter for whom the decision was certainly the hardest – each was prepared to 'let their parents go'.

India had been pioneering work, the national movement was in its infancy and OM precipitated the wave of Indian Christians. When they moved to Pakistan, they again were involved in pioneering work, preparing the ground for the national believers to continue. Now they are moving to Central Asia, to a country where there are no church buildings, but there are 'secret' believers.

John and Leena will be going to an area where there is no running water, no electricity and little heat. It will be a tremendous challenge after the comforts of home – but to Leena in particular it is a vision realised after many years as this country has been in her heart since she was a teenager and heard a missionary speak about the country.

In preparation for the work, John and Leena have spent three months in an intensive training programme becoming qualified to Teach English to Speakers of Other Languages (TESOL) as this will be their main area of service, running language classes for nationals and government workers. Even this is a big step as teaching is one area that John has always been reluctant to get involved in, but once the Lord showed him, on various visits that they have made, the strategic nature of this work he realised that this is the way forward.

Once they arrive they will be undertaking another intensive six month language course, before embarking on their teaching programme. The main area of evangelism will be low key, building relationships, making the most of hospitality and opportunities to show the realities of Christ to the local people.

They are really looking forward to getting involved in the work – anticipating being involved in establishing a national movement as in the past. "We are getting back to what makes us tick", says John "and we are excited and motivated to make the most of the opportunity to break new ground in this pioneering situation".

The country that John and Leena are going to can be danger-ous, but they are prepared to put up with the hardship and difficulties to follow the Lord's call. They were not prepared to sit back, even though they were already involved in the Lord's service. We can all learn from their example – the Lord may not be calling us to Central Asia or even to a foreign country; but He may be calling us to leave our comfort zones if we are prepared to truly follow Him. Think on those words that greatly affected John so many years ago and still impact his life today – so much so that he and Leena are now serving the Lord in difficult and potentially dangerous circumstances, just so that those who have not heard the gospel even once get an opportunity to discover the truth about the Lord Jesus Christ.

*"No-one has the right to hear the gospel twice until everyone has heard it once."*

# CONCLUSION

As I draw this book to a conclusion, it is time for me to declare my hand. I am another one of those Englishmen who have been mightily blessed with a Northern Irish wife. I have been involved with Christian work over the last 12 or so years in a variety of ways. Most recently with Christian Care Trust which seeks to bring care and support to churches in Southern Romania, one of the poorest regions of that still needy country. We run camps for children and young people and support practically and financially the work of the churches in reaching out into their villages. Having the privilege to visit Romania a couple of times each year, has, I believe, been life-changing and working with those Christians who have been through so much has been a source of constant amazement and blessing.

I am also involved in local church leadership and strive to encourage others to look outside of their comfort zone, as it were, and seek God's leading as to how they can get involved in and outside of the local church.

There you have it: twenty different testimonies of ordinary people that God has used over the years. Some have only served for a short time; nevertheless the impact on their lives has been immense. Others have committed themselves for the long term, even up to 50 years, but believe that any sacrifice that they have made has been worthwhile through all of the ups and downs. Some people like only to work in the background, not taking the limelight and just serving with the gifts and skills that God has given them.

We have seen people of all ages and all backgrounds ready to take a stand and serve the Lord. We have seen God call them under different circumstances and we have seen them go to different countries across the world and some have stayed in Northern Ireland. We have seen people who have undertaken all kinds of service, using their gifts and talents in a wide variety of ways. We have seen that God sometimes calls people as children, at other times when they are older. We have seen that even those who have reached rock bottom can be raised up to serve and we have seen that tragedy can be turned into triumph in God's hands.

What is it that is stopping you from getting involved?

God can use anyone who is ready to take a step of faith. Let me urge you to discover more; contact one of the organisations that are listed in the appendix or any other that you know of yourself. Jesus said: 'The harvest is plentiful but the workers are few. Ask the Lord of the harvest, therefore, to send out workers into his harvest field.' (Matthew 9:37-38)

Perhaps you are one of the workers that have yet to go.....

**YES YOU CAN!**

# APPENDIX
Mission Organisations' Websites
(of the workers in the book)


| | |
|---|---|
| Child Evangelism Fellowship | www.cefireland.org |
| Christian Care Trust | www.romaniacare.org |
| G.L.O. | www.glo-europe.org |
| I.F.E.S. | www.ifesireland.org |
| Kyles (e-mail address) | alankyle@online.fr |
| M.E.C.O. | www.aboutmeco.org |
| New Tribes Mission | www.ntm.org.uk |
| Operation Mobilisation | www.uk.om.org |
| O.M.F. | www.omf.org.uk |
| People International | www.peopleintl.org |
| Project Evangelism | www.projectmh.org |
| S.I.M. | www.sim.co.uk |
| World Gospel Mission | www.wgm.org |
| Wycliffe Bible Translators | www.wycliffe.org.uk |